# ISRAEL:

SO-AET-905

G. Allen Fleece Library
Columbia International University
Columbia, SC 29203

# A Secret
# Documentary
# by Lance
# Lambert

**Tyndale House**
Publishers, Inc.
Wheaton, Illinois
Coverdale House
Publishers, Ltd.
London, England

G. Allen Fleece Library
Columbia International University
Columbia, SC 29203

Library of Congress
Catalog Card Number:
75-7230
ISBN 8423-1803-8, paper
Copyright © 1975
Tyndale House Publishers, Inc.
Wheaton, Illinois 60187
All rights reserved
First printing:
July 1975
Printed in the
United States of America

# CONTENTS

# INTRODUCTION

Israel expected the Day of Atonement on Saturday, October 6th, 1973, to be as quiet as usual. It was not. In fact, it saw the beginning of the most serious of Israel's wars. Many regarded this as just another Arab-Israeli squabble. Was it? Would it have mattered if Israel had lost? Is the preservation of the State of Israel of such importance and significance?

I had always found the American Colony Hotel the most gracious place in Israel, and a friend and I were thoroughly enjoying the last few days of our holiday. It had been the most peaceful vacation that we had spent in Israel. We had particularly noticed how relaxed everybody was, including the Arab population in Jerusalem and on the West Bank. Our return flight to England was booked for the following Monday, in two days' time.

Suddenly the air raid sirens wailed all over the city. My immediate reaction was to wonder whether this signaled the holiest part of the Day of Atonement. However, I quickly realized that this could not be, because the strict laws for the Sabbaths and for holy days would normally have ruled out the use of sirens, and this Day of Atonement was both a Sabbath and a holy day. While I was still pondering this, the sirens wailed again. Israel's fourth war had begun.

On the Bar-Lev line along the Suez Canal, a bored Jerusalem Brigade swatted flies and slept. Many men were keeping the fast. Some played a slow game of soccer. When someone kicked the ball to the top of a bulldozed rampart of sand, a private went after it. Looking out over the Canal, he was shocked by what he saw. "MIGs! MIGs!" he shouted, as Israel came under attack from 200 Egyptian fighters.

On the Golani Heights, eighty Israeli soldiers were enjoying a day of leisurely military duty. Some were still playing backgammon and wearing their slippers when four Syrian helicopters filled with assault troops swung around a mountain. Many Israelis were killed in hand-to-hand fighting in the bunkers. Other surrendered, only to be executed.

Israel had become overconfident since her last confrontation with her hostile neighbors. She was taken by surprise. With the Arabs united for the first time for many centuries, equipped with the latest weapons and confident of victory, it appeared that this tiny nation with such a rich religious heritage would be destroyed. Yet God had not forgotten his people.

This was the Yom Kippur War—a modern-day miracle of deliverance by the God of Israel.

# ABORTED
# ANNIHILATION

The Yom Kippur War should have been the annihilation of the State of Israel.

People think of the 1967 Six Day War as a miracle, and it was. It was nothing, however, compared with the Yom Kippur War. In the years that lie ahead, when the whole truth comes out, we shall find that it should have been the end of Israel. It was a miracle of the very first order that Israel was not annihilated.

A few weeks after the war, I heard Golda Meir say, "For the first time in our twenty-five year history, we thought we might have lost." Before then I had never heard an Israeli personality so much as imply the possibility of defeat. I had never heard them admit to fear. That was the first time! At one point in the war, only ninety battered Israeli tanks stood between the powerful Egyptian army and Tel Aviv. Yet Israel was not beaten.

The Yom Kippur War of October 1973 marked a new point in world history. Things will never be the same again. The First World War was another such turning point. With that war a whole order of things passed away, much more so than with the Second World War, which only finished off the process. The First World War changed the face of Europe and the world. Reigns, kingdoms, and monarchies disappeared. New ideologies arose. Marxism had its birth in that era. In a similar way the Yom Kippur War, far from being some petty Middle East war, was one of the great milestones of history.

Yom Kippur in Hebrew means "Day of Atonement." Among Latin and Oriental Jews (the Sephardim) this Jewish holy day is also called "the Day of Judgment." On this day Jews pray particularly for forgiveness, and ask that their names be "written and sealed into the Book of the Living."

On the Day of Atonement everything in Israel is at a standstill. From two hours before sunset until two hours after the succeeding sunset everything stops. There is no transportation —no taxis, no cars, no buses, no planes, no trains, no ships. The nation's airports are closed, the ports are closed, the stations are closed. No shops are open, no entertainment can be had anywhere. There are no radio programs, no television, no communication with the outside world and very little within Israel. Even the telephone exchanges are not staffed on the Day of Atonement. It is a day of prayer and fasting, spent either in the synagogue or at home.

Israeli Intelligence knew all about troop movements in both Egypt and Syria, but the signs were misinterpreted. These two countries have military maneuvers in September and October every year. There had been a general Israeli mobilization in June that same year, and that mobilization cost Israel $9,600,000 per day and tore over a third of the manpower out of the economy. So now General Dayan, along with the Israeli Cabinet, thought that these troop movements were just a war of nerves, a bluff to produce another mobilization with the accompanying paralysis of the economy and tremendous financial drain.

Israel thought of Anwar Sadat, the president of Egypt, as a "weak sister" and was confident that the Arabs lacked the unity necessary to mount an organized attack. The possibility of a new war was recognized two weeks before it actually began, but as government officials later admitted, "The Minister of Defense knew of enemy concentrations, but he could not accept the verdict of immediate war." Shimon Peres, then Minister of Transport, said, "We did not want to believe our own Intelligence, we did not want to believe that Sadat was going to do it." It was 4 a.m. on the Day of Atonement before it was realized that something very serious was afoot.

A United Nations representative, who had already proved to be very accurate in the information that he passed on to his Israeli counterpart, had information that in the course of the Day of Atonement, Israel would be attacked on two fronts. This warning was taken very seriously indeed when it was finally relayed to Israel, but by then it was too late. It takes at least forty-eight hours for a full mobilization of the Israeli Defense forces. By seven o'clock that morning the military authorities had started to recall men on leave, but it was only two hours before the war began that most of the men were contacted and the reserves mobilized.

On this particular year the Day of Atonement was more generally observed than ever before. A large number of the men on the fronts were actually observing the fasting and prayer. Synagogues all over the country were filled with people, most of them men. This was somewhat unusual.

Our first public warning that something was wrong came when the air raid sirens wailed for about three minutes at 2:10 p.m. and again at 2:20 p.m. Within fifteen minutes Israeli radio was on the air broadcasting live reports from both fronts. You could hear gunfire and explosions in the background. These sirens were, in fact, the only means the Israeli government had of informing the nation that something very serious had happened. Husbands and fathers, brothers and sons were called suddenly from synagogue or home. They had only a few minutes in which to say good-bye. The majority of them thought it was a short skirmish, such as they had had before. They left hurriedly, fully expecting to come back. Three thousand of them never returned, and many more thousands were maimed for life.

It was a massive and terrible onslaught on both fronts. There were more tanks on the Syrian front than in the 1941 German offensive against Russia. That offensive was 200 miles long and involved 1,000 tanks. On the Syrian front, the Golani Heights, there were 1,200 tanks on a twenty-mile front. The greatest tank battles in world history were later fought in the

Sinai, greater even than the battle of El Alamein in the Second World War.

In Britain we are at times still a little imperialist in our attitude. We had tended to think of Syria as a tinpot Middle East state that one only had to blow at and she would fall flat. Syria, however, hit Israel with more tanks in that initial attack than Britain and France possess together. Indeed, one high-ranking English officer in a tank regiment told me that Britain and France have only one-third of their tanks actually ready for use in the event of an attack at the present time. Approximately 4,000 tanks, 900 missile batteries, and even unproved new weapons were thrown into action right at the start of the Yom Kippur War. It was the first wholly technological war in Middle East history.

I quote from Abba Eban, former Foreign Minister of Israel, in his statement to the United Nations on October 8th, 1973: "Egypt attacked with 3,000 tanks, 2,000 heavy guns, 1,000 aircraft, and 600,000 men."

Against Syria's massive tank attack, the regular Israeli garrisons numbered only a few hundred men in all. The Egyptians, with their greater numbers, should have been in El Arish, if not in Gaza and Beersheba, within twenty-four hours. There was nothing to stop them. Israel was not armed to the same extent as her Arab neighbors because the U.S. Pentagon estimated that Israel's manpower was technologically superior, and therefore did not need to be comparably equipped.

The Arabs, however, had weapons not only

in greater number than the Israelis, but also in many cases far superior. They used hand-held missiles such as the RPG7, which can blow the turret right off a tank, and the Snapper, a mobile anti-tank rocket, which makes tanks burn so fiercely that the armor melts. They also had SAM 6s (surface to air missiles), antiaircraft rockets that travel at two and a half times the speed of sound. At six miles range this gives a pilot only fifteen seconds in which to take evasive action. In the early stages of the war three out of every five Israeli jets were shot down. In those first few days Israel suffered terrible casualties.

The Bar-Lev line fell, the Hermon fortress was taken. Both of these had been thought in the popular mind to be invincible. The Egyptians crossed into Sinai, and the Syrians took much of the Golan. The Israeli news service had until then always been most reliable. It might interest you to know that many Arabs tune into Israeli Arabic broadcasts for accuracy. During the first week of the war, however, Israeli news tended to be very inaccurate, and news from Damascus and Cairo much more reliable.

This was largely due to a breakdown in communications between the front and second lines of defense on the Israeli side. Even Moshe Dayan was confused on the second day of the war because of this. Whole companies and units were wiped out without a survivor. Yet, on the whole, morale on the Israeli side was very high, especially at the front.

Egypt and Syria should have beaten Israel,

but they were inexplicably stopped. The Egyptian high command gave the first Egyptian division that crossed the Canal fifteen hours to take the Bar-Lev line. They took it in just five hours, and then stopped. If they had swept on, the whole of central Israel would have been at their mercy. One Egyptian tank commander said later, "I was only half an hour's drive from the Mitla Pass, and there was nothing to stop me." But he stopped.

Likewise the Syrians should have been in Tiberias on the evening of the first day of the war, but they too stopped. The commanding officer of Israel's Golani brigade said later in my presence that when the Syrians were first advancing, the Israelis had only two tanks and ten men at their Golani headquarters. This man was not a believer in God, nor in any way religious, but he said that this was a miracle. In none of the four wars of Israel's history, all of which he had been involved in, had he ever seen anything like it. Wave after wave of tanks bore down on them. Then, when they came to within one mile of the Golani headquarters, they stopped. He put it very humorously. He said, "They saw the Lake of Galilee, they liked the view, and they stopped."

These delays in the advances of the Egyptian and Syrian forces gave Israel time to regroup and reorganize. Many feel that it was this time that made the difference in the outcome of the Yom Kippur War.

An Israeli captain, again totally irreligious, said that at the height of the fighting on the Golan, he looked up into the sky and saw a great, gray hand pressing downwards, as if it were holding something back. In my opinion that was exactly what happened. Without the intervention of God, Israel would have been doomed.

Shimon Peres, once a key adviser to Golda Meir and the present Minister of Defense, has said, "The miracle is that we ever win. The Arab nations occupy eight percent of the surface of the world. They possess half the known oil resources and are immensely rich. They have more men in their armies than we have people in our state, and on top of the Arabs come the Russians, who have built for them a great war machine. On our side we have only America."

It was at this point in the war that I first learned of the massive Soviet airlift of arms to Syria and Egypt, which had begun on the first day of the war. Large numbers of Antonov transport planes carrying weapons and replacements began arriving just two hours after the war started. One was landing every three minutes. At the same time that the war began, Russian ships arrived at Latakia, Syria, and Alexandria, Egypt, carrying heavy military replacements for everything that was going to be lost in the war. Three days before the war began the Soviet Union launched two orbital Sputniks, which crossed Israel at the best time for aerial photography. Russia then relayed information to Syria and Egypt as to whether Israel was prepared. This is why the war was originally planned for six o'clock in the evening of Yom Kippur, but was moved up to two o'clock. The Russians had passed on the information that preparations had begun on the Israeli side.

The American airlift did not begin until the tenth day of the war. Each plane carried 100 tons of ammunition, tanks, and weapons. The Israeli army was actually running out of ammunition by the time the airlift began. The delay was almost completely caused by the refusal of America's so-called allies, particularly Britain, to grant facilities to the United States for refueling her planes. Britain was so bitter about the airlift that she persuaded her NATO allies to fight it. Germany refused to allow the United States to take weapons from her bases on German soil and put them on Israeli ships in Bremen and Hamburg. Finally Portugal opened up the Azores to United States transport planes, and Israel was saved. Planes then came in almost nose to tail. There was no time to lose. If they had not come, Israel would have been totally lost.

The fighting became increasingly severe. Galilee was shelled, and the Syrians even used Frog missiles. There were many air raids in the north. Then gradually Syria was pushed back. Meanwhile, Egypt was held in the Sinai. The greatest tank battle in world history was fought there on Friday, October 19. Much of the fighting was at such close range that they were not even able to maneuver the tanks. Jordanian radio described it as "hell on earth."

The so-called "even handed" British and French embargo on arms was in fact loaded against Israel. Many of the weapons captured by the Israeli defense forces were British. I saw some of these with my own eyes. This means that they were coming from Kuwait into Syria. Britain supplied Kuwait with arms throughout the war. Two French Mirage fighters were shot down and captured by Israel. There are only two nations in the Mediterranean which use Mirages—Israel and Libya. Libya, supposedly a nonbelligerent, was supplied by France with planes and weapons all the way through the war. She obviously passed on this equipment to Egypt. The French embargo on Israel, moreover, was so bitter that she would not even allow blood donated by French volunteers to be sent to the Israeli wounded.

Israeli British-made Centurion tanks were immobilized through lack of ammunition and spare parts. Some tanks went to the front under their own power, rather than being transported, so their tracks were damaged by the time they arrived there. Spare parts and ammunition had already been paid for, but were on board Israeli ships in British ports when the embargo was placed on them. The entire cargo was impounded by the British government. There would certainly have been an outcry in Britain if India, for example, had taken the same action with ships flying the British flag.

Many nations joined Egypt and Syria. In the first twelve days Saudi Arabia, Kuwait, Yemen, Iran, Sudan, Libya, Morocco, Algeria, Tunis, and Jordan all joined in on the Arab side. North Vietnam sent a contingent of pilots to Syria. In the first two weeks of the war, twenty-seven African states broke off relations with Israel. Many of them were the recipients of Israeli aid. Thirty-four states in all, including India, broke off relations in this way. Other countries, which were supposed to be impartial, were in fact bitterly hostile to Israel—for example, Malta.

The growing isolation of Israel can be seen in all this. People sometimes wonder how Armageddon could ever take place. This war proved that within a few days contingents from all the armies of the world could be in Israel.

Furthermore, with the exception of the moderator of the Church of Scotland, no church leaders condemned the fact that the war was a premeditated attack on the most sacred day in the Jewish calendar. The Israeli Cabinet felt very bitter about this. Some of them said, "We never expected Christian churches to support us in the war, nor would we ever expect Christian churches to collect money for ammunition or weapons. We did not even expect them to collect money for our wounded. But we thought that the least they could do was to stand up and say that they thought it was a terrible thing that on the most sacred and holy day of the Jewish calendar, when everyone was fasting and praying, this premeditated attack took place."

The Pope just talked about the need for peace on both sides, and said that one could not blame the Arabs for longing for their old homelands. The World Lutheran Federation remained absolutely silent, as did the Anglican Church. The World Council of Churches sent $2,000,000 worth of aid to Jordan, and an undisclosed sum to the Palestinians, which probably means the terrorists. Until that time the World Council of Churches had never sent even one dollar to Israel. However, because of bitter complaints from church bodies within Israel, for the first time in its history it sent five and a half tons of medical equipment there!

A friend of mine, who is an Anglican clergyman in western England, asked the secretary of the British Council of Churches whether this information were true. He was told, "I am sorry to say that it is. You must understand that of course there are no Jews represented on the World Council of Churches, so there is no Jewish voice to say anything." The secretary added, "We also have a growing left-wing, radical influence in the World Council of Churches, and I am sorry to say that they outvote the rest of us." He also mentioned that the sum sent to the Palestinians exceeded the $2,000,000 sent to Jordan.

The International Red Cross recognizes the Red Crescent in Arab lands and the Red Lion and Sun in Persia, but refuses to recognize the Red Star of David in Israel (Magen David Adom). I have a copy of a letter dated 1972, in which the president of the International Red Cross states that "the leadership of the IRC did not think it appropriate to give attention to the case of the recognition of the Magen David Adom at this stage because of the well-known political difficulties involved." In an International Red Cross Congress held in late autumn 1973, there was a two-thirds majority vote of censure on Israel's conduct in the war.

An incident occurred at Lod Airport when Egyptian prisoners were being taken back to Egypt, all of them stretcher cases, and they were held up because two of the stretchers had the Red Star of David stamped on them. For one and a half hours the authorities searched the whole Tel Aviv area for two stretchers without such markings. Finally they sprayed something over the Red Star of David, and only then would the officials of the International Red Cross accept the prisoners.

Many of the Christians in Jerusalem felt that the main reason that the Lord was keeping me in Israel was for prayer. Living in a house in the Garden Tomb, which many believe to be the site of the resurrection of Christ, I was at the heart of things. This is the natural center for most of the believers in Jerusalem. The burden we had was for real prayer. I found here, as everywhere else, that corporate prayer was a lost art. So many believers know how to pray personally, but they do not know how to pray together.

I was appalled that when Israel was in such great need, even missionaries who had been truly called of God and burdened for the events of the hour were unable really to pray together. It was not that these believers were necessarily divided on personal or doctrinal issues. It was a question of the lost art of corporate prayer. We therefore held a school of prayer at the height of the war. Our burden was for the dying and wounded, Arab and Jew alike, that they might be saved; for the Israeli people, that the war might be used to turn them to God; for the invaders, that the Lord would paralyze and confuse them; and especially for Jordan, that she would not enter the war.

The administrator of the Garden Tomb is Colonel Orde Dobbie. His father, General Dobbie, defended Malta during the Second World War. He is a true Englishman, not given to fantasy or too much excitement. On the third day of the war he had a vision. Early in the morning, while he was praying, he saw himself on the Mount of Olives. Then he saw great clouds roll out of heaven down onto the Mount of Olives and from there across the wilderness of Judea, blotting out the whole country of Jordan. It was so vivid that he immediately turned in prayer to the Lord and said, "Lord, what does this mean?" He felt that the Lord replied, "Pray that the Jordanian authorities will be so confused that they do not enter the war."

He came to me early the next morning and told me about the vision, and asked, "Do you really think that it was of God?" I felt that it was. We felt quite sure that we must give ourselves to much prayer that day, that clouds would come down upon King Hussein and the Jordanian Cabinet. We also prayed that believers would be protected and used at both fronts and at home.

We had some remarkable answers to our prayers. Jordan stayed out of the war. Officially they sent a token force, a crack regiment called the 40th Brigade. However, the 40th stayed behind a hill on the Syrian front, and never fired a shot. Indeed one Israeli general felt that they were there to stop the Syrians and

Iraqis from entering Jordan, rather than to fight the Israelis. The bridges over the Jordan River were open for civilian traffic for almost the whole war. They were closed only three times in four months, and that on separate occasions.

We had the tremendous joy of hearing King Hussein being interviewed in English on a radio broadcast. The Indian interviewer said, "You are very unpopular with quite a number of the Arab states, because they feel that you have let down the Arab cause, and that if you had opened the third front, Israel would have been finished." And incidentally, Israel *would* have been finished. Hussein replied, "Well, they may feel that. I can understand it. But you see, we were very perplexed the day the war began and ever since, for we do not feel that we have sufficient air cover to allow us to attack. And we are not sure that we would have gotten the support that we needed from Iraq and Syria." That was a great answer to prayer. He actually used the word "perplexed."

We continued to pray that the Lord would confuse the invaders and cause them to hesitate; and that the nation might be called to repentance and prayer, which would have been a miracle. We prayed for the Israeli Cabinet, especially for Golda Meir, then seventy-six years of age. Mrs. Meir was an atheist but later became an agnostic, and at Ben-Gurion's funeral in 1973, she actually said, "I thank the Almighty that two years ago he brought about reconciliation between me and David Ben-Gurion." I had never heard her refer to the Almighty before as such. She sometimes uses the expression "Thank God" for this or for that, but only as a colloquialism.

We prayed that the hidden motives and counsels of the Soviet Union might be unmasked before President Nixon and the Free nations, and that President Nixon's impeachment at such a time might be averted. We prayed that he would give up the two tapes, which at that time he did not want to give up. We prayed that the Egyptian Third Army would be surrounded and even surrender, thus bringing a speedy end to the conflict.

We had some remarkable answers to these prayers too. For the first time in Israeli history, one of the three leading rabbis of the Jewish Agency sent out a letter appealing for repentance on the part of the Jewish people. He listed fifteen reasons for the need of this repentance, including Israeli car driving—if you have experienced this, you will understand why!

The Egyptian Third Army was surrounded and cut off, and became dependent upon the Israeli forces for food and medical supplies. The Israeli army punched a hole in the Egyptian defenses and poured over the Canal into Egypt. Syria was pushed back to within fifteen miles of Damascus. President Nixon gave up the two tapes, and his impeachment was averted.

On Sunday, October 21st, Henry Kissinger was urgently called to the Kremlin. The next day there was an unofficial cease-fire on the Suez front. We felt that this could be to Israel's grave disadvantage. We remembered that, under cover of the 1971 cease-fire, the Soviet Union had supported Egypt in the moving up of SAMs to within one mile of the Suez Canal. These ground to air missiles, which were never taken away in spite of much fuss and bother in the United Nations, nearly determined the course of this war.

Why was it that Britain and France did not seek a cease-fire when Egypt and Syria were on Israeli-held soil? President Nixon had personally asked the then Prime Minister of Britain, Mr. Heath, if he would propose a cease-fire resolution in the United Nations Security Council, but Mr. Heath had refused. As soon as Damascus and Cairo were threatened, however, Britain moved with amazing speed in order to get a cease-fire resolution passed. We prayed that the cease-fire might be broken if it was only going to allow Egypt and Syria to rearm and regroup for more bloodshed.

The Egyptians broke this unofficial cease-fire three times. On the fourth occasion, the Israelis punched back. They went as far as Ismailia and then turned southwards, cutting off Suez City and ending up only fifty miles from Cairo. Earlier a retired colonel in the Israeli army had told me, "I have lived here all my life. I am a *sabra* (native-born Israeli). Every time we have had one of these cease-fires, they have not kept it. We report it, and report it, and report it, and then we just have to fight back. That is what will happen this time. They will probably break it three times, and the fourth time we will punch back and take all the territory we need." That is exactly what happened, and it made Russia furious. Brezhnev sent Nixon what Senator Henry Jackson called "the most brutal cable ever sent to a President." Later the United States State Department said, "Well, that is rather emotional language to use about a cable. It wasn't really as bad as that."

But what Brezhnev said in this cable was that the Soviet Union had decided to take unilateral action and so resolve the Israeli problem. America took this very seriously, because American reconnaissance flights had already spotted a large Soviet warship not only heading for Alexandria, Egypt, but actually docked there. On the deck of this warship were ballistic missiles with nuclear warheads. At the same time, the Soviet airlift dramatically stopped, and all those huge transport planes were at the ready while crack Soviet parachute regiments moved towards the airfields. Aware of both these facts, President Nixon, thank God, called a worldwide United States military alert, a Stage Three alert in the five-stage American Defense Condition. This put 2,300,000 men on standby and was the first such alert since the Cuban crisis eleven years before.

Why did the Russians bother to cable Nixon? Why not just get on with the job, let the Egyptians have a ballistic missile, and let them fire it? Why tell the Americans? I asked a high-ranking Israeli expert on foreign affairs about this. According to him, the Russians believed that they must observe some outward form of detente. They believed that Nixon was in such a domestic mess at that point that he would delay at least twenty-four hours, by which time Egypt would have fired two or three ballistic missiles and wiped out Haifa, Tel Aviv, and probably western Jerusalem. When the dirty deed was done and there was worldwide protest, Russia would hold up her hands in horror, and say, "We are very sorry, but what is done is done. Israel is finished." Thank God that, in spite of his personal and national problems, Nixon proved to be quick-witted and sharp. Surely this was of the Lord.

I had a very interesting confirmation of this, for those of you who know something about prayer. Samuel Howells, principal of the Bible College of Wales and son of Rees Howells, the great intercessor, told me later that one of the greatest times of prayer that he remembers since the war years came on the night President Nixon called the alert. During that day he had felt a tremendous burden and anguish come upon him. He walked up and down, prayed for a while, and in the end asked the Lord, "What does this burden mean?" The Lord told him, "My enemy is seeking to precipitate Armageddon." Then Samuel Howells spent some time in prayer. Later, during the course of a regular evening meeting, he and others felt led by the Holy Spirit to remain in prayer until early the next day.

The next morning they were not surprised to hear about the worldwide United States military alert. However, they did not realize the full situation until I was able to explain it to them some months later.

At approximately the same time, thousands of miles away from Wales, Gladys Thomas and Kitty Morgan were praying in Israel. They had learned some of the deep lessons of intercession with Rees Howells during the Second World War. As they prayed that day the Lord had said to Gladys, "Pray! For my enemy is seeking to precipitate the end."

Throughout the world many thought that the United States alert was ordered for domestic reasons. Believe me, it was not. At that time we came to the very brink of World War Three. In Britain and Europe, hardly anyone realized it. We were living in a fool's paradise, teetering on the brink of nuclear war. Believers in the Free World were quite unaware of the grave issues at stake at that time. They continued their routine meetings and programs, oblivious of the tremendous movements in the unseen world. Our Lord told us to watch and pray, to be ready for the things coming upon the face of the earth. Were we ready then?

As soon as the United States worldwide military alert was called, the Soviet warship weighed anchor and sailed back to the Black Sea. Israel's annihilation had been aborted.

# 2

## HOW LONG PEACE?

What has happened since the cease-fire, signed on November 11th, 1973?

By June 1974, military personnel from Yugoslavia, Russia, and other Eastern European countries, as well as from North Korea, North Vietnam, and Cuba, had arrived in Egypt and Syria to supervise the more sophisticated weapons given to them by the Soviet Union. Seven hundred fifty Cubans are manning a tank brigade in Syria. There are over 3,000 Russian advisers at operational level in the Syrian armed forces. The Russians are manning ground to ground missiles, and installing ground to air missile launchers. Forty-eight North Korean pilots are on active duty in the Egyptian air force. East Germany has sent pilots and electronic warfare specialists.

Syria has become one vast arsenal. Her readiness for war has doubled, some would say trebled, since October 1973. Furthermore, the Iraqi armed forces have received 1,000 T-54 and T-62 tanks. They have also received various missiles, including Frog ground to ground missiles, and 350 planes, including the new Tupolev 22 long-range bomber. There are now between 1,000 and 1,200 Soviet advisers in the Iraqi forces. There are so many Soviet advisers in Somalia and Aden that they could actually close down the Bab el Mandeb Straits, and so block the whole Red Sea to shipping should they so wish.

At the Rabat Conference in October 1974, a fighting fund was set up by the oil-rich Arab states placing $1,000,000,000 a year at the disposal of Egypt, Syria, Jordan and the Palestinian Liberation Organization (PLO). Another $70,000,000 per year was given to South Yemen to establish a major Arab military base at the Bab el Mandeb Straits.

In the autumn of 1973, Dr. Joseph Luns, NATO secretary-general and Dutch ex-foreign minister, warned the NATO foreign ministers concerning the Soviet Union's intentions with these words: "I feel very much like I did in 1936-37, watching the Nazi war machine build up while they signed peace treaties and made pacts taking in most, if not all, of the governments of Europe." He went on to warn them: "Countries do not equip themselves with vast armaments and devote enormous resources to the acquisition of vast military strength if they do not contemplate exploiting it." While the Warsaw Pact countries and NATO countries have been talking of forces and weapons reduction, the Soviet Union and her Eastern European allies have been involved in an unprecedented military buildup.

The former British foreign secretary, Sir Alec Douglas Home, patched up a quarrel between Britain and the Soviet Union over the expulsion of 100 spies some years ago. He recently returned from Moscow, however, to tell the same NATO foreign ministers' conference not to sign a forces and weapons reduction agreement at the present time. What changed his mind? At the same conference Max van der Stoel, the present Dutch Minister for Foreign Affairs, said, "We have to ask ourselves if the Soviets did not perhaps put the Arabs up to using the weapon of oil to undercut the economies of the industrialized West. Indeed, we in NATO have to find out if the Soviets did not instigate the Arab attack on Israel itself."

The oil embargo was agreed upon by the Arab oil-producing states in January 1973, nine months before the war began. Holland was selected for a total embargo at the same time. Two-thirds of Western Europe's oil is refined in the port of Rotterdam, Holland.

What about the disengagement? I must say that I think it is a tragedy. On the short term side, it seems wonderful. At least the Israeli prisoners have come back from Syria, and the Syrian prisoners have returned to their families. It is also good in the sense that war has ceased, the shooting has stopped, and lives are not being lost. However, it is in fact short-term peace and long-term escalation.

I was in Israel during the whole course of the disengagement talks with Syria. Dr. Kissinger was flying every day to Damascus from Jerusalem, and then back again in the evening, and at one point it seemed that the whole thing would break down. Russia had an interest in preventing the disengagement from succeeding. Why? The United States is working overtime to get Egypt, Jordan, and Syria into her camp, and away from Russia's. The U.S. is caught in the middle. She must support Israel because of the large and powerful Jewish population in America. Yet she cannot afford to be anti-Arab because of her growing need for Middle East oil, and her $3,000,000,000 investment in Arab oil production.

Even if Israel withdrew, a third world war would be inevitable, because the United States would have to guarantee the Israeli frontiers and the Soviet Union the Arab frontiers. There would then be the real possibility of a superpower confrontation. The Americans are fully aware of this. They are putting colossal pressure on the Israeli Cabinet to withdraw, and this means that they know they have to guarantee Israel's boundaries. What they are trying to do is get Egypt, Syria, and Jordan into the American camp, as well as Israel. This would enable them to act as guarantor to both the Israelis and the Arabs, rather than having the Russians on one side and themselves on the other.

It is reasonably clear so far that Dr. Kissinger is succeeding in getting Egypt and Jordan into the American camp. Syria, however, is another matter. The Soviet Union tried to disrupt the disengagement talks, and rumor has it that there were two assassination attempts on Kissinger while he was in Damascus. It is widely believed in Israeli government circles that these were the result of Russian KGB activities.

Do not be deceived into thinking that this

disengagement is the first step in peace. It is not. Israel has lost every advantage that she so dearly fought for with the lives of her sons. The disengagement zone in the Golan is so narrow, deliberately, that the Syrians can fire right over the United Nations forces into Israel.

Mount Hermon is the most strategic military strongpoint in the whole of the north. From its summit you can see the whole of the road to Damascus, and you have not only a commanding view of the Golani Heights and all southern Lebanon but also all of upper Galilee. On a clear day all military maneuvers can be spotted from this peak. Israel was particularly interested in regaining the Mount Hermon fortress, and all three peaks of Hermon. She held two peaks, but the highest peak of all, the peak that actually overlooks Damascus, was not held by Israel before the war. She obtained it through bitter fighting. Indeed, relatively more men were lost in the battle for the Hermon peak than in any other campaign in the war. In the disengagement, however, the Hermon peak was taken away from Israel and went under United Nations control. This is a pathetic position for Israel. It means that the Syrians can build military posts all around the United Nations area of control. All Syria has to do then is to order the United Nations out, and the United Nations would have to go. They cannot hold the area.

There are a number of other disadvantages to the cease-fire. Syria refused to officially guarantee that terrorists would not act against Israel from Syria. It was felt in Israel that if

Syria really wanted peace, she would have guaranteed this. Why then did Israel agree to a cease-fire with such humiliating disadvantages for her? I asked an Israeli expert on foreign affairs about the Hermon peak. He said that it was a total waste of life, and indeed all the loss of life on the Golan front was apparently wasted. I then asked him, "Isn't it better to keep fighting, rather than agree to something which is so much to your disadvantage?" He replied, "No, we cannot do anything else, because of the pressure that Kissinger is putting on us."

Kissinger, although he later denied it, implied that the United States would withhold economic aid unless Israel was prepared to withdraw from "occupied territory." Israel therefore agreed to give back the Hermon peak, to withdraw from Syria, and for the first time to give up territory already settled by Israeli settlers on the Golan, that is, the El Quneitra triangle. El Quneitra is a ghost town which was once the market center for the whole of the Golan.

Nevertheless Syria still is not satisfied. She wants back all of the Golan. Many have accused the old Israeli Cabinet of a tactical error in giving back El Quneitra, because it means that Israel has now no more ground to give back. If she surrenders any more, the whole of Galilee will be at the mercy of Syria. From the Golani Heights they could fire down upon all the settlements in northern Galilee. It is therefore Syria that is thought of in Israel as the real threat, not Egypt.

It is widely believed that Egypt wants peace, certainly far more than Syria does. Why? Egypt wants to reopen the Suez Canal. She wants to make Port Said a great tourist center. Egypt has been rebuilding Port Said, and the civilian population has already begun to go back there. Egypt may therefore really mean what she has said about ending hostilities. Moreover, Israel is able to negotiate further with Egypt about Sinai. There is much more of Sinai which Israel is prepared to surrender to Egypt than there is of the Golan to give back to Syria. If Syria demands that she move back, Israel is almost forced to refuse. That is why she wants to talk with Egypt next, in order to avoid this confrontation with Syria.

We are beginning to see a very interesting regrouping in the Middle East. Egypt, Jordan, and Saudi Arabia are gradually moving together into a block, which is for peace on certain terms. Certainly Egypt is moving towards the American sphere of influence, and away from the Russian. On the other hand, Syria, Iraq, Libya, and the Palestinian Liberation Organization are becoming more and more adamant in their demands, and have moved further into the Soviet camp.

Could Israel have won the Yom Kippur War? I do not think that the Israeli defense forces ever thought that it would be feasible to take either Damascus or Cairo. The reason, of course, is that it would take a large number of men to govern such antagonistic populations. At the same time, the general feeling was that Israel was robbed of a decisive victory by Kissinger's diplomacy. The Israelis had the Egyptians on the run. Surrounding them and bringing them to surrender would have meant a decisive victory. Kissinger believed, however, that Arab pride would only make such a humiliating blow ground for further war.

Will the war be resumed? King Hussein, interviewed on the BBC at the beginning of this year (1975), solemnly warned that unless the lost momentum for peace is quickly regained, war is inevitable and would be a disaster for the whole world. The Israeli Prime Minister, Yitzhak Rabin, has said, "We must expect the resumption of war from the north, that is, from Syria." Probably the first sign will be that Syria will order the United Nations out of the buffer zone. Israel's new policy appears to be that the moment that happens, she will make a preemptive strike. Of course that would incur the wrath of the Third World and much of the Western world.

What will Israel do about the missile problem which caused her to lose so many planes in the Yom Kippur War? I am not a technical expert, but I understand that a number of Israeli planes have been fitted with a new chiming device, to track incoming missiles. We must remember that the Yom Kippur War very quickly became a trial run for a third world war. The Soviet Union began to send in all kinds of new weapons in order to try them out under conditions of actual war. Even the Pentagon did not know of the existence of some of these. For example, there is no equivalent in the West to the latest SAM missiles. Then too there were the mines in the Gulf of Suez, which neither the American or British navy, nor the Israeli navy, were able to neutralize. They had to call in the Soviet navy to do this, because the West had no equivalent mines. The Yom Kippur War was therefore a kind of testing ground for new weapons.

Along with the other problems confronting Israel is the specter of insolvency. It cost Israel $240,000,000 for every day between October 6th and November 11th, 1973, and since then $9,600,000 for every day of general mobilization to the present time. The threat of renewed war and continual terrorist activity both outside and inside Israel have reduced her tourist earnings, her most important means of gaining foreign currency. It is now apparent that the Arab intention is to keep up the war atmosphere in order to drain away Israel's life and smash her economy. When she is at her weakest, the Arabs can deal her a death blow. This plan appears to be working very successfully. With a spiraling inflation of seventy percent, recrimination as a result of the war, and a good deal of industrial discontent, Israel is facing insolvency. Humanly speaking, her future is bleak. The enormous military resources of her neighbors, the rapidly expanding Arab wealth, Israel's growing isolation, the aloofness (if not coolness) of her former friends, her dwindling foreign exchange, and the inevitability of war, all spell Israel's collapse.

There is, however, in this dark and gloomy scene one ray of hope. That ray is like the morning star that shines in the darkest part of the night to herald the coming of a glorious dawn. It is the Word of God. For Israel is now the cornerstone of world politics, and will be to the end of this age. She is God's object lesson. Through Israel God reveals that history is not a tangle of confused strands, but that in it he is working all things according to the counsel of his will. In Zechariah 12:2, 3, 6, God says, "I will make Jerusalem and Judah like a cup of poison to all the nearby nations that send their armies to surround Jerusalem. Jerusalem will be a heavy stone burdening the world. And though all the nations of the earth unite in an attempt to move her, they will all be crushed . . . In that day I will make the clans of Judah like a little fire that sets the forest aflame—like a burning match among the sheaves; they will burn up all the neighboring nations right and left, while Jerusalem stands unmoved" (TLB). That is the one thing we can say. Come what may, Jerusalem will be where Jerusalem has ever been, because God has decreed it.

I, of course, deplore the fact that so many lost their lives in the Yom Kippur War, but I thank God that it is one of the means by which he is driving that nation to himself. God is bringing Israel step by step and stage by stage to the recognition that they don't have sufficient resources within themselves with which to face the future, and that they must therefore look elsewhere. Their growing isolation among the nations means that they cannot depend on any other nation. The plan of God is in this. Something tremendous is happening.

# OUT OF PAIN,
# PRAYER

Syria threw 1,200 tanks into the attack on the Golan. Only 240 returned. The Israeli defense forces, however, had only seventy tanks on the Golan when the attack came. The Israelis fought almost with their bare hands. Most of the soldiers were between eighteen and twenty-one years of age. Many were still fasting, having had no food or drink for nearly twenty-four hours. Most of the men on both fronts were young conscripts, because the rest had been allowed to go home to their families, especially those who had been on national service for more than a year or two.

General Rafoul described the way the Israelis held back the Syrians on the Golani Heights in these words: "We stopped the Syrians by the sheer heroism of soldiers refusing to give way. Each man understood that the choice was either to stand and fight it out, or allow loved ones in the valleys behind them to be slaughtered in case of a full breakthrough."

There were many true stories of boys who shot down enemy airplanes. This all began with a Tel Aviv taxi driver, twenty years of age. When one of the MIGs came in low, shooting everything up, and everyone else dove for cover, he fired his machine gun and the plane blew up. It then became quite a popular pastime to see if one could knock planes out of the sky. The same was true of the tanks. One lad was very badly wounded, so that eventually his foot had to be amputated. The tracks of his tank were damaged, but not the gun. The other crew members were critically wounded, but he was in a position to be able to train the tank gun upon each Syrian tank as it came up over the brow of the hill. He knocked out sixteen tanks before he was himself put out of action. We heard many such stories.

I remember meeting a boy who was one of only three survivors in a unit of fifty at El Qantarah. There was another boy who was the only survivor out of 250. In Ein Kerem, a suburb of Jerusalem and the birthplace of John the Baptist, there was scarcely one family that did not suffer bereavement. One of the reasons for this was that it is Israel's policy to send boys from the same area into the same regiment. It is considered to be good for morale. This means that boys who have grown up together and have gone through school together, go into the same regiment together. This is all very well, when they do not get killed. However when the fellow with whom you grew up dies alongside you, it is a terrible shock. This is why in a place like Ein Kerem there was hardly a family unaffected. The whole unit from that area was wiped out.

Israel is unique in that it does not keep its

officers in the rear of the battle. They lead their men, following the Old Testament tradition. It is always sad that some of the best young men lose their lives in each of these battles. You can imagine some of the sorrow and sadness. An Israeli mother asked, "Would you pray for my son? He is out of his mind. He will never be normal again, so the psychiatrists say, short of a miracle." When most of his unit were either killed or badly wounded, he and two others decided that the only thing to do was to surrender. They were completely surrounded. They laid out two rows of very badly wounded men, one of sixteen or seventeen and the other of eleven. They put out a white sheet to signal their surrender. It was accepted, and the three men were told to stand to one side. When they did this however, the Egyptian tanks moved forward and crushed both lines to death. Twenty-four hours later the boy went out of his mind, and, as far as I know, he is still in that sad condition today.

A taxi cab driver was at a hospital, having taken some friends to visit their wounded son. While there, this man saw one of his son's friends, who told him, "I am very sorry, but your son is dead." The man decided to go straight home and tell his wife the news. When he got home he found a cable informing them that the elder boy had also been killed. The father collapsed with a heart attack, and died.

An official in the foreign ministry told me about a friend of his, a totally irreligious man, who came in and said, "Have you got a prayer hat?" "Yes," he replied, "why?" The friend said, "I want it. Don't ask me why. I will tell you later." The official eventually found out that this man's only son had suffered severe brain damage because of shrapnel. The doctor had said that if the boy recovered, he would be a mere cabbage. The father had never prayed before, but he went to his son's bedside and prayed for nine hours that God would take him. After those nine hours, the boy died.

I remember the case of another lad. He had come close to suicide. He was on the Bar-Lev line and was badly shot up. He did not know how many hours he had been unconscious, but when he regained consciousness lying in a pool of his own blood, he realized that he had no legs and thought that he had no arms. So, making a great effort, he tried to turn over so that he would roll down into the Suez Canal and drown. As he rolled over, he suddenly realized that he still had one arm attached to his body, although badly wounded. This stopped him, and he decided to live. That boy was being rehabilitated, along with many other severely wounded men. There are many such stories, but I do not just want to recount harrowing stories for their own sake. It is sufficient to say that there was very, very great sadness throughout Israel.

There were other remarkable stories too. There was the Hebrew Christian who was called up nineteen times by the military authorities at the wrong address. Finally his whole unit of 250 went to the front line without him, and there was not a single survivor. Because of an official mix-up, this Hebrew believer survived.

The medical care was amazing. It took on the average only six hours to get a man from the front line to a regular hospital. The new policy of the Israeli government is to send doctors with their orderlies right into the front lines. You may have seen this on television news reports. Men were shown being brought out with intravenous apparatus already in them. Many of the boys still able to walk, actually walked up to the helicopters holding their intravenous equipment because there was such a scarcity of manpower. I am afraid, however, that although many thousands of lives were saved by this policy, a number of Israel's finest young doctors lost their lives.

The Hadassah Hospital at Jerusalem performed 581 major operations around the clock in the first twenty days. At their field hospital under canvas, 100 major operations were performed in the first twenty days, and these included the most delicate brain surgery. These operations were on men who were too ill to be moved by helicopter into the regular hospitals.

Those in the United States have learned something about burn injuries from the Vietnam War. The Yom Kippur War certainly had its share. New weapons pierced tank armorplate and then burst into flames, roasting people alive inside. One must also remember that tanks carry their own ammunition, which explodes when the tank is hit. The Hadassah

Hospital had a whole top floor given over to burn cases. I was deeply moved by what I saw and heard when I visited the hospital. The professor taking me around told me, "Many of these boys are unrecognizable as human beings. They have melted." Most of them were only eighteen or nineteen years old, with the whole of their lives before them. Those with medical experience will know that such burn cases suffer terrible psychological aftereffects. Later the professor in charge of the Burns Unit told me that out of sixty or more cases with full-thickness burns (every level of skin tissue being affected), only one died. This is a remarkable tribute to the loving devotion of the doctors and nurses there, who worked day and night to save lives.

On a recent visit to the hospital I saw one of these survivors. He had returned there for plastic surgery and further rehabilitation. He was nineteen years of age, and must have been a good-looking young man. His face now looked as if it had completely melted—no eyebrows, no eyelashes, hardly any lips, and two dark brown eyes looking out from what appeared to be a grotesque mask. Even his hands had melted into grotesque shapes. The professor in charge told me that they had even been able to tell at what time of day the boys had received their burns. At night they were only burnt on their faces and hands, but during the day, especially at midday, the burns were far more extensive because the boys had rolled up their sleeves and opened up their shirts.

Pray for these boys, that they might find God. I was so deeply moved by all this that I told the authorities that we would make ourselves responsible for rehabilitation equipment. It has since been my joy to be able to channel over $14,000 worth of rehabilitation equipment to Hadassah for the use of these boys. Some of them will need care for virtually the rest of their lives.

I have been amazed at the effect that our small gifts have had. On a return visit to Israel, I met all the professors of Hadassah, and one after another said, "We have had some very big gifts, but it was these small gifts from groups of Christian students in Britain and Norway that deeply touched us." The thing which touched them most of all was that a group in the eastern section of Jerusalem also gave something. Some of this group were Arab Christians. This particularly impressed the Israeli medical authorities, because they remembered that in the 1948 War of Independence, a medical convoy had been ambushed by the Arabs in that very part of the city. Many leading professors and doctors were killed in that ambush. Now after all these years, in a time of need, Arab believers in that same area had joined with other Christians in giving this money.

There were also many cases of paralysis resulting from the Yom Kippur War. There are men who will be lame, or dumb, or blind for the rest of their lives. There were also many terrible brain injuries, and of course there was much shock, severe shock, as a result of which many cannot speak or see. This was the first war in Israel's twenty-five-year history that resulted in such severe cases of this kind. If there was no other evidence, this would be enough to show what kind of war the Yom Kippur War was. Several of the boys told me that what shocked them most was the fact that the Egyptian troops had been given a drug, something like LSD, which made them completely impervious to fear. Colonel Amnon Resheff, commander of Israel's 14th Armored Brigade, said, "Our task was made more difficult by the human waves coming at us. It did not seem to matter how many we killed, they kept on coming. The attacks they made were often suicidal. Their commanders did not care how many perished."

During the whole course of the war I did not personally hear of one Hebrew Christian killed or even wounded. I did, however, hear of many who had significant opportunities to serve their fellow Israelis on both fronts. One believer from Tel Aviv, named Haim, was on the Sinai front, and he had his Bible with him. A big topic all through the Israeli army at that time was biblical prophecy. Many were asking, "Have the Old Testament prophets said anything about the days in which we are living?" Most of these boys knew nothing about the Bible, and nothing about prophecy. Whenever they found someone who did, they wanted to hear from him.

Haim was in great demand everywhere. After the first two weeks of the war, there was a little more free time, and the boys would gather around and discuss these things. They would say, "Now you read it to us. Where is it?" Then Haim would lead them in a discussion about the Scriptures. One of the funniest stories I heard was of a jeep driving up at great speed, and two fellows jumping out of it and running into the mess hall.

"Where is Haim? We want Haim."

"There are lots of people called Haim. Which Haim?" the men in the mess hall answered.

"We want the Bible Haim."

"You cannot have him, he stays here."

"We want him down at our end of the Canal, because we have great discussions going on, but no one has a Bible, and no one knows anything about these things."

At the very height of the war, Arab and Hebrew believers were praying together in Jerusalem, and this was a miracle. Even more miraculous was the fact that those working among the Arabs and those working among the Jews got together. The great breakthrough came after a slight confrontation in one of our times of prayer. First someone prayed for Israel and the Israeli Cabinet. Then someone prayed equally seriously for the Arabs "for whom our Lord had also died." I immediately stopped the prayer meeting and said that if we were going to pray horizontally like this and shoot one another down in prayer, we might as well stop altogether. I mentioned that I thought the breakthrough would come when one of those working among the Jews, and wholly for them, prayed for the Arabs, and vice versa.

The change did indeed come when someone who was fanatically pro-Israel prayed that the Arab wounded would really find the Lord, and for Arab believers in Damascus that they might be helped by God at that time. That brought us all together, and from then on we trusted each other and were able to pray for Arab and Jew alike without recrimination.

The war deeply affected some of the Israeli leaders. Golda Meir, seventy-six years of age, went to the airport nearly every day on which there were prisoners returning from Egypt, and waited hours to be able to greet them. There were only a few hundred of them in all. At times she wept so much that the television cameras had to be turned away from her. Other times, after a twenty-four hour Cabinet session or something similar, she would go to Hadassah or Tel Hashomer and visit the wounded boys, instead of getting some sleep.

The Israeli military authorities often showed humanitarian concern for the welfare of their enemies. I heard about the Syrian pilots who parachuted out of their planes into the sea. It was not the Lebanese government, nor the Syrian, but the Israeli authorities who sent launches out to rescue them. I was told of an incident when the Israelis found the body of a Syrian pilot who had been left unattended within shouting distance of his own units. He had bailed out of his plane, and was wounded in his arm and thigh. They were relatively superficial wounds. However he was left to bleed to death when he could easily have been saved by his own troops. On his parachute he had scrawled in Arabic, in his own blood, "Allah help Syria, if this is the way she treats her sons."

Most of the Israeli prisoners of war in Egypt were tortured. Some of them will never walk again because of the things which were forced into their bodies. I will not go into the details. I will, however, tell you this. At the Hadassah Hospital one of the leading brain specialists in the world, an Israeli, performed a $4,000 operation on an Egyptian major and by so doing saved his life. This surgeon's own son will never walk again, because of the way he was tortured by the Egyptians. At the time of his capture he could walk perfectly.

The idea that Israel is an imperialist, colonialist state with a kind of *apartheid* is absolute nonsense. At the Hadassah Hospital, whose standards compare favorably with leading hospitals in London or New York, an assistant surgeon and one of the chief nurses are both Arabs. They work alongside their Jewish colleagues quite happily. After all, Jews and Arabs are cousins. One third of all the out-patients at this hospital are Arab, and about a quarter of the in-patients. There is no distinction made between the two. One cannot help but feel that forces outside the country are playing on this whole matter. If it were not for these outside forces, Arab and Jew would probably live in peace.

I remember speaking with one of the world's leading dermatologists at Hadassah. He was a specialist in leprosy, and he told me, "If you want to know the funniest story I have, here it is. Just before the war a woman came to us from Cyprus, an Arab woman, and she had the first signs of leprosy. She asked if I could treat her. I said, 'Yes, have you any money?' She said, 'None at all.' So we put her on government expense. During the following months, the fact emerged that her husband was an officer in the Jordanian army, which was facing the Israeli forces. She was totally cured, went back to Jordan, and promptly sent a friend to us who also had leprosy, to be cured free of charge at Hadassah."

There are many signs of very deep moving in the Israeli nation. Golda Meir said, in a speech which I found one of the most moving I have ever heard, "There is no Jew in Israel who can say that he is the same today as he was on the eve of Yom Kippur. I don't believe I will ever be the same." Bibles and prayer books were in demand above all else by the soldiers. Indeed, this had its amusing side. In the Hebrew press a controversy raged, as to whether the field rabbis (service chaplains) had failed in their duty or not. The crux of the complaint was this—there had been a run on Bibles during the first few weeks of the war, and there were none available.

Who could blame the Jewish chaplaincy, however? For years no one, except perhaps one lad here and there, had ever asked for a Bible. Now suddenly thousands of men wanted them. One Israeli entertainer took a whole truckload of vodka, Bibles and prayer books to the Golan to distribute to the soldiers. It was very cold there, and he took the vodka to try and keep the boys warm. Surprisingly enough, however, it was not the vodka they wanted, but the Bibles. By the Bible, of course, we mean the Old Testament. But do not be worried about that. The early church only had the Old Testament. Some people think that without the New Testament, it is impossible to find God as Savior. This is not true, as the early church proved. The New Testament is, of course, necessary for the full revelation of God's plan of salvation, but the Old Testament is also the Word of God which lives and abides for ever.

A recent report of interviews with soldiers has revealed that a most amazing percentage of them went into the war as atheists and came out as "believers." They are not believers as Christians understand the word, but believers in a Supreme Being. That is nevertheless a tremendous change of heart. One man told me, "I have never seen anything like it. The boys prayed before battle, during battle, and after battle. They spent time reading the Torah (the first five books of the Bible), and discussing it. I have never seen anything like it. Women normally pray, but not men."

One great joy was the fact that the Israeli Cabinet officially sanctioned fifteen minutes of Bible reading on the Israeli radio. This had never happened before. The Bible is read for fifteen minutes during prime listening time each evening.

On November 5th, 1973, a few days before the cease-fire, miracle of miracles, the chief Rabbi called Israel to prayer. That was the first official day of prayer that modern Israel had ever had, and the whole nation went to prayer. The synagogues were packed with people. There were never less than 3,000 at the Western Wall in prayer, and it was real prayer from the heart.

# 4

## A SEARCHING NATION

There are some evangelical Christians who seem to think that all Israelis are children of God, that angels hover over the street corners of Tel Aviv, and that miracles are performed daily throughout Israel. Nothing is farther from the truth. There are probably as many prostitutes in Tel Aviv as there are in Soho, London, or in the slums of any large American city. There are also the usual number of racketeers and swindlers.

Israel is by and large an irreligious nation. Perhaps I ought to explain what I mean by using the adjective "irreligious" in this connection. There is in Israel a small but vocal and influential religious minority. There is also deep within the Jewish heart a religious awareness. Nevertheless, modern Israel is the product, humanly speaking, of early pioneers who were for the most part radical socialists and agnostics. There are a few religious kibbutzim, but for the most part, the kibbutzim are irreligious from an Orthodox point of view. They observe the festivals and fasts as national holidays, rather than for their religious significance. Nearly all the members of the Israeli

Cabinet are either atheists or agnostics, excluding of course the National Religious Party member. There are only two others, so far as I know, who even vaguely believe in a Supreme Being.

In all the years that I have been traveling to and from Israel, and even during the months of the Yom Kippur War, I have never known the Israeli people to be so depressed and despondent as I have found them recently. A pall of depression, almost one of death, hangs over the whole nation. This affects everyone from the young people in the streets to the high officials in the government. Even people who are normally vivacious and full of humor seem to be under some sort of cloud.

Israel feels that she is no longer free to make her own decisions. Her policies are largely being dictated by the Pentagon and other outside forces. She is under pressure to accept conditions which she does not believe are for either her own good or for the good of the Free World. She is trapped in the web of superpower politics.

Added to this is the fact that Israel lost 3,000 of her finest young men in the war itself, and a further 180 died in the ensuing fighting on the Golan. For a nation of only two and one-half to three million people, that is a colossal proportion to have lost. By comparison Syria and Egypt have a combined population of 40,000,000, and so are more able to bear their losses. If we were to translate the Israeli figures into American terms, it would mean a loss of 200,000 lives. You can imagine the mourning, sorrow, and sense of emptiness which would hang over the

United States if she lost 200,000 young men in a few weeks.

However, the enormous death toll is not the only factor causing this national despondency. There has also been a tremendous amount of inner disunity and recrimination as a result of the war. This actually began during the war itself, when two generals began to argue with one another in public. These were the aggressive General Ariel Sharon and Major-General Shmuel Gonen, whom many feel was promoted beyond his ability. Of course the quarrel was partly political in origin. Most of the other generals are socialists, and Sharon belongs to Likud, the liberal-conservative party.

The whole Israeli nation has gone on a kind of orgy of national introspection, investigation, and recrimination. Many who have lost sons, husbands, brothers, fathers, have been asking whether the government did not let them down. This was the first time that Israel had ever been taken by surprise, and it is becoming increasingly clear that only a miracle prevented the Arabs from winning the war. Naturally this has shocked the nation, as has the somber fact that the majority of those who died were in the units that were overrun during the first two days of fighting. There were hardly any survivors from these units. Those bereaved are charging the government with criminal negligence. I am not at all sure that they have the truth on their side, but this is their charge.

As a result of all this, David Elazar resigned, and Mordecai Gur, another general, took his place as Commander-in-Chief. This may be good for the country. Moshe Dayan, of course, also stepped down, and I am sure that this will be to Israel's loss. Golda Meir finally resigned because of the inner disharmony, backbiting, and bickering in her coalition of left-wing parties. At her age she eventually found it all too much of a strain. It was sad to see someone who had served her people so valiantly and sacrificially, leave office in these circumstances. So Yitzhak Rabin became Prime Minister. He was something of an unknown quantity when he took office. He had been an army general and a very successful ambassador to the United States. He is a highly intelligent and capable man, and is proving to be a strong and resilient leader.

Probably the biggest shock that Israel received was at the end of May 1974, when it became public knowledge that the United States had concluded an agreement with Egypt the previous January to give her a nuclear reactor. At no time had Kissinger acquainted any member of the Israeli Cabinet with this decision. President Nixon, Dr. Kissinger, and Joseph Sisco, a long-time United States negotiator in the Middle East, have all said on a number of occasions that American policy towards Israel has not changed. This is just not true. It has undergone a colossal change. The change lies not so much in America's dealings with Israel, as in her dealings with Israel's neighbors. She is seeking to bring Egypt, Jordan, and Syria into her orbit of influence, and so cannot give Israel the same kind of support as previously. Obviously the development and maintenance of friendly relations with these Arab nations must have an effect on America's attitude to Israel herself.

I believe that all this has something to do with Israel's present spiritual condition. She is beginning to feel totally isolated, even from her one staunch and faithful friend, the United States. The United States has rearmed Israel and will continue to rearm Israel, but the Common Market nations are not going to help her, and neither are the nations of the Third World. The United States is her only friend, and therefore has the upper hand. She pays the piper and she can call the tune. Israel knows full well that Kissinger has only to withhold her desperately needed economic aid, or to refuse to sell her the latest weapons, and that would be the end.

In addition to this is a sense of hopelessness and despondency that the last war, which should have finished up with Damascus and Cairo at Israel's mercy, instead saw the whole Israeli triumph taken away from her by American intervention and pressure. Israel now feels that in winning, she did not win. In fact, she was robbed of a first-rate victory that could have shattered the invading armies and rendered them inoperative for at least five years. With hostile armies not only intact but rearmed, with no added security (in fact, far less), and with so many dead, naturally her people are asking, "Was it all worth it?"

When we gather all these strands together, we can begin to understand the despondency which has settled upon the Israeli people. The nation's growing isolation, the inevitability of renewed war, the specter of insolvency and economic ruin, the inner disharmony and recrimination resulting from the war, the enormous resources of wealth in the Arab nations arrayed against her, the Soviet Union's undisguised hatred and the likelihood of her coming into the next round of fighting—all of this more than explains the despondency and depression.

What is the spiritual condition of Israel now? I do not believe that great military triumphs on their own would ever bring the Jewish people to Christ. These only foster their sense of self-assurance. We can well understand such self-assurance, for it has been produced by the tough, pioneering spirit which owes no man anything. It was this independent self-sufficiency which turned arid deserts and malarial swamplands into fields and gardens. Israel has had to fight the whole way. Basically no one supported those early settlers. A large number of them died in the process, but others carried on until finally the orchards, vineyards, and farms of modern Israel took shape. Not only in the early days, but all the way through her history, Israel has had to fight for her very existence. This spirit of proud independence and self-sufficiency has resulted in a certain amount of arrogance and cockiness.

The military triumphs of the last twenty-five years, moreover, have only increased this. It is the kind of spirit that said, "You only have to fire a few shots in the air, and the Syrians run like rabbits. You only have to point a tank in the direction of Cairo, and the Egyptians collapse immediately." All that has now disappeared. Israel has lost her arrogance, and the Yom Kippur War is the reason. That war and its aftermath have made Israelis realize that they need some kind of moral strength and power which they do not have in themselves. The fact that their one great friend, the United States, appears to be withdrawing and taking up a new and more impartial position, means that the Israelis feel somewhat bereft and insecure. I believe that for the first time Israel is beginning to feel her need for some kind of power beyond herself. She has not lost her courage nor her will to fight, but she has started on an inner quest. That quest will end in a discovery of the living God.

When I visited Christian friends in Jerusalem recently, they told me that they had never before had so many inquiries from young Jewish people as at present. The attitude of Jewish Russian immigrants is an encouragement too. Some of them are believers. In the Soviet Union Jews have been as much oppressed as Gentiles in the matter of religion. It is as much frowned upon to go to synagogue as it is to go to chapel or church. Everyone there grows up in an atheistic environment. The Jews are very conscious of being Jewish. They respect their background, but they also have to listen to endless discussions about the worthlessness of religion. In spite of this some have found the Messiah. Being Jewish they have applied for visas to come to Israel as Jews. This is tremendous, because it means that they are fully accredited Israeli citizens. At the Garden Tomb in Jerusalem, whole groups of Russian Jewish immigrants have been coming to see the site. These people have a tremendous interest in the Messiah and talk freely about biblical prophecies. They are representative of some 3,000,000 Jews in the Soviet Union. Let us pray that those 3,000,000 will participate in something similar to the Exodus from Egypt.

The many complex and insoluble problems confronting the Israeli people at the present time are undoubtedly being used by God to force her into a new position. The Lord is cornering Israel. Step by step, and stage by stage, God is shutting up Israel to himself. In the end there will be no way out except through him. Israelis are beginning to look at their own history to rediscover the inner significance of their survival. I believe that this is the first sign of the Holy Spirit's new working among the Jewish people.

## GOG AND
## MAGOG?

During the Yom Kippur War all Israel was talking about Gog and Magog. There are two old Jewish gentlemen, a Mr. Schwili and a Mr. Shiloh, who have written at different times independent articles on the biblical prophets, with particular regard to the numbers given by them. Using rabbinic methods these men came up with a series of past and future dates important to Israel. The dates are: 1880, 1917, 1948, 1967, 1973-74.

Their findings would by no means meet with the approval of the majority of Bible scholars, and should be evaluated with very real caution. Although both these men were interviewed at various times on Israeli television and radio, and articles appeared about their findings in newspapers and magazines, they were never taken seriously. They were regarded as lovable eccentrics. Of the two, Schwili is the more reliable. They published the results of their work in books and pamphlets in Hebrew, the latest in 1968.

Of course 1880 was a remarkable date in the history of Israel, because it marked the first great wave of immigrants (especially Ukrainian and Russian-Polish) out of which a whole number of settlements and cities arose. For example, Rishon le-Zion, Petah Tikvah, Degania, Rosh Pinna. 1917 saw the Balfour Declaration of a Jewish homeland. In that document Arthur James Balfour, the British foreign secretary, declared that "His Majesty's Government views with favour the establishment of a national home for the Jewish people, and will use their best endeavours to facilitate the achievement of this object." In 1948 there was the re-creation of the State of Israel against overwhelming odds. 1967 marked the return of Jerusalem to Jewish administration and control for the first time in 2000 years, with the exception of some months in A.D. 135. Schwili and Shiloh agreed in principle upon 1973-74 as the year when the war of Gog and Magog was to occur.

I must say that in all the years that I have been traveling to Israel, and I am generally there for at least two months each year, I have never known Israel more relaxed or peaceful than in August and September 1973, just before the war. One could drive along any of her borders without problem. At one point I nearly drove over into Lebanon by mistake.

Suddenly, on the Day of Atonement of all days, and without warning, the worst and most severe of Israel's four wars began with a massive attack on two fronts. The Israeli people began to talk. Many of them said, "Do you remember that old man who was interviewed on television? Didn't he say something about 1973-74?" Others remembered what the newspapers and magazines had printed about the two men's findings. Everywhere people began to talk about Gog and Magog.

Soldiers on both fronts were asking whether the Hebrew prophets had said anything about the present conflict or what was to follow it. Teachers told me that even children came up to them and asked, "Would you please tell me about Gog and Magog? What is it?" As Christian teachers are not allowed to influence minors in religious matters, one teacher, when asked that question by a child, sent him home to ask his parents. The following day the little boy came back and said, "My parents say they want to know what Gog and Magog means too."

There are few subjects on which such widely differing views have been held than on the subject of Gog and Magog. Very much controversy has been generated by it. It would be well for us to exercise extreme caution as we approach such a matter. For instance, we should, I think, be careful about Schwili and Shiloh's dates, as we should also be about some of the more extreme interpretations of chapters 38 and 39 of the book of Ezekiel. Personally I feel that much damage has been done by those prophetic systems that spell out all the details. To give such a dogmatic and detailed sequence of events is dangerous. There is nothing wrong, however, with a personal view, provided it is open to correction and further revelation. The greatest tragedy of all is when we make our view of prophecy the ground for faction and division.

So often these matters are revealed to us as they happen. For instance, Jerusalem was taken by Israel in 1967. At that time I said publicly in a number of places, "Now we must wait and see. If in a year's time Jerusalem is still under Jewish control, we will know that the prophecy of our Lord in the Gospel of Luke has been fulfilled." That was in 1967. Jerusalem has not only remained in Jewish hands, it has been unified under an Israeli administration. I think that that event has given us a very real key to a number of other prophecies. The same was true of the re-creation of the State of Israel in 1948.

We can especially learn about the Gog-Magog prophecy from Ezekiel 38 and 39. Chapter 38 mentions a number of names—Gog of the land of Magog, prince of Rosh, Meshech and Tubal (vv. 2-3), Persia, Cush, and Put (v. 5), Gomer and Togarmah (v. 6), Sheba, Dedan, and Tarshish (v. 13). It is interesting to find a number of these names linked together in Genesis 10:2-4. Gog could be a person or a people. Magog in Hebrew is literally "of Gog" or "from Gog." It is probably the name of a place derived from Gog. It would appear that originally Gog and Magog were associated with Asia Minor. The prince of Rosh could as easily be translated "the chief prince of Meshech and Tubal." Rosh in Hebrew means "chief" or "head", and is so translated in the King James Version and other translations. Some would identify Rosh with Rash, a place west of Elam, modern Iran. It is interesting that in Hebrew the letter *aleph* is used, although we now pronounce the word "rosh." This could point to "rash" being the original pronunciation.

Meshech and Tubal are found linked together

throughout Scripture. See Genesis 10:2, and Ezekiel 27:13; 32:26. Both were located east of Asia Minor. Persia presents no real difficulty, although it covered a larger territory than modern Iran. Cush is normally understood as Ethiopia, but was more centered on modern Sudan than modern Ethiopia. Put is often identified as Libya, as in the King James Version. This identification is possible, but it is more probably modern Somalia and Eritrea in East Africa. Gomer is to be located north of the Black Sea, Togarmah in Armenia, and Sheba and Dedan in modern Saudi Arabia, south and north respectively. Merchants of Tarshish were Phoenicians originating in Tyre and Sidon, modern Lebanon. All these names, barring the last three, are seen as actually involved in the planned invasion of Israel. Sheba, Dedan and the merchants of Tarshish stand to gain much, as less involved collaborators.

There have been widely differing views as to the identification of these names with modern nations. For example, there is the widely held view that Rosh is to be identified with Russia, Meshech with Moscow, Tubal with Tobolsk, and Gomer with Germany or Eastern Europe. While this view cannot be reliably supported, we must note that three times it is stated that the invading forces will come from "the uttermost parts of the north" (Ezekiel 38:6, 15; 39:2). Note too that in Ezekiel 38:6 it is Togarmah that is mentioned in connection with the uttermost parts of the north, but in 38:15 and 39:2 it is Gog. Note that the modern versions rightly translate this as the "uttermost parts" (RSV), "the remote parts" (NASB), and "the far recesses" (NEB). The King James Version ("north quarters," "north parts") is not accurate here. It is not good enough to say that this phrase meant the northern fringe of the known world at that time, that is Armenia, and cannot mean anything beyond the Caucasus. The prophecy was given for the understanding of those living in the last times, and to them the uttermost north must mean just that.

Another small but interesting point is that the name Ashkenazi (see Genesis 10:2-4) is the name given in modern Jewry, through long usage, to all Jews originating in northern and central Europe speaking Yiddish, that is those from Russia, the Ukraine, Poland, Germany, etc. All Jews originating in the south, that is Oriental and Latin Jews, are called Sephardim.

A far more important point is that nearly all the invasions in Israel's history have been from the north or from the south, hardly ever from the west or the east. These invading nations may not have been geographically situated in the north, but in the east, such as Babylon and Persia. In the war described by Ezekiel the nations may likewise come from many quarters, but they will invade from the north and it is there that this whole confederacy of evil will be militarily centered.

What we can say with some certainty is that Ezekiel, by the Spirit of God, used these names to symbolize powers north, south, east, and west of Israel, nations hostile to the purpose of God. He appears to predict a gathering of these nations led and armed by certain northern powers. He also implies, if he does not actually state, that the invasion will be from the north. (See Ezekiel 38:15; cf. v. 9.) Gog and Magog appear in early Jewish literature after Ezekiel's time as symbolizing in general the leaders of world powers hostile to God and his purpose. Many Jewish sources since have regarded Gog and Magog as describing northern barbaric nations. As early as the first century after Christ, Josephus, the Jewish general and historian (c. A.D. 37-100), identified them with the Scythians. These were themselves a nomadic tribe originating in western Siberia and living between the Black and Caspian Seas. In general usage the name "Scythians" came to describe any number of northern barbaric tribes controlling the steppe lands and trade routes of Russia. Many identify the Scythians with the Ashkenaz.

Have we any clear indication as to when all this is to take place? Once again there are widely differing views. Very much depends upon whether one believes that the reference to Gog and Magog in Revelation 20:8 is to the same war as in Ezekiel 38 and 39. If one believes that it is, and that there is to be a Millennium, then it must come at the end of it. There are, however, real difficulties here. Ezekiel 38 and 39 refer to an Israel which has been regathered and re-created as a nation. Yet there is no mention of the Messiah as present in their midst, and we are told that the Holy Spirit will be poured out upon them after this war. (See Ezekiel 39:29.) Furthermore, it would appear that the war takes place after the re-creation of the State of Israel, but before all Jews have been regathered. (See Ezekiel 38:8; cf. 39:28.) None of this fits the usual Millennial view.

Just because contending nations meet together in battle in the Middle East does not mean Armageddon is upon us, not even if the point of contention is Israel herself. Undoubtedly there will be a number of serious battles over Israel, involving many nations. They will not necessarily be Armageddon. In one sense there may well be a number of "mini-Armageddons." We have several examples of this principle in Scripture. For instance the words of our Lord about the destruction of Jerusalem (Matthew 24, Luke 21, Mark 13) were not exhaustively fulfilled in the city's destruction in A.D. 70, but appear to await a further and final fulfilment.

We have further examples of this in the Old Testament prophecies which had their first fulfilment in the return from Babylon, and yet were not exhaustively fulfilled then. Perhaps this principle is most clearly seen in the matter of the Antichrist. Daniel's prophecies concerning him were first fulfilled in Antiochus IV Epiphanes (c. 163 B.C.). Antiochus became the archetype of Antichrist in Scripture. Down through the years believers have seen the Antichrist in a number of historic personalities. For example, Nero, Napoleon, Hitler, Mussolini, Stalin. All these men were "mini-Antichrists" in so far as the spirit of Antichrist was in them. They were all to a greater or lesser degree demon-inspired. The final Antichrist will sum them all up, entirely eclipsing them.

In the same way it could be that we shall have several "mini-Armageddons," when the nations of the world collide over Israel. In my estimation the war in Ezekiel 38 and 39 could well be one of these.

Does the reference in Ezekiel 38:11 to "unwalled villages" give any indication of time? Many would say that Israel is like a fortress at present. Can we say that Israel is "at rest" or "dwelling securely" (v. 11)? In the whole twenty-five years of modern Israel's history she could hardly ever have been termed "at rest." On the other hand, one has only to speak to older Israelis, who have known the pogroms, the Nazi era, and the ghettos, to hear them say that the present era in fact spells comparative security and freedom for them. It is also only in the last century that there have been unwalled cities, towns and villages in Israel.

One thing is very clear from Scripture; at the very point when it seems that Israel will be destroyed, there will be an intervention from heaven and the whole of the military confederation from the north will go up in smoke. Israel will spend seven months burying the dead. That confederacy, having planned to finally solve the Israeli problem by her complete annihilation, will itself be wiped out. Whether the miraculous intervention of God will be a divinely-timed earthquake or something nuclear, I do not know. It is a real possibility that, as has happened so many times in the history of the people of God, the enemy's own weapons will backfire on him. The very means by which he has planned to destroy Israel could come back on him. A ballistic missile, for instance, could fall short and destroy the whole northern confederacy. What we do know is that they will be destroyed by divine intervention, in a single moment of time.

It is a very sobering thought that God has said that he is not only going to send fire on Magog, but also on "those who dwell securely in the coastlands" (Ezekiel 39:6, RSV). In the King James Version the word "coastlands" is translated "isles." The Hebrew word was originally used to describe the islands of Greece, but came to mean all that lies beyond Israel to the west. What does it mean that God will send fire on the coastlands? Surely it means that in some way the western world will be involved in this "blowup" in the Middle East.

Let's summarize the points upon which there is some certainty:

1. This planned invasion of Israel is at the time of the end, the last part of the age. (Ezekiel 38:8, "latter years," literally "end of years"; Ezekiel 38:16, "latter days.")

2. Israel is again dwelling in the land, i.e. Israel is re-created as a state. (Ezekiel 38:8, 14.)

3. There is a gathering of nations against Israel from all sides—north and south, east and west—but the attack is from the north. (Ezekiel 38:1-6, 13; 39:2.)

4. The phrase "uttermost parts of the north" is mentioned three times. (Ezekiel 38:6, 15; 39:2.) There must be some meaning in our at-

tention being drawn to not just the north but to the uttermost parts of the north.

5. Reference is made to the fact that these nations will be armed to a quite exceptional degree. (Ezekiel 38:4; 39:9, 10.)

6. The destruction of this great armed confederacy is by divine intervention. (Ezekiel 38:18-22; 39:3-10.)

7. The destruction takes place upon the mountains of Israel, and is colossal and final. It will be the end of the northern powers. Ezekiel 39:2-20.)

8. It would appear that more than the Middle East is to be affected by this war and God's intervention in it. (Ezekiel 39:6. Note "the coastlands" or "the isles.")

9. It will result in the final ingathering of the Jewish people to Israel. (Ezekiel 39:21-28.)

10. The Holy Spirit will be poured out upon them after the war. (Ezekiel 39:29.)

In my view the stage is now being set for a military catastrophe over Israel which will be of real consequence to the rest of the world. Whether this will be the Gog and Magog war of Ezekiel 38 and 39 or not is open to question. As I have already stated, there are many interesting features developing in the present Middle East situation which could link it with Ezekiel 38 and 39, but it would be foolish to be dogmatic over this. The next war, though serious, may only be part of the buildup. Whether the Gog and Magog war described by Ezekiel comes within the next year or the next decade, it will come and it could all happen in a moment.

# WILL ISRAEL
# SURVIVE?

"The conflict in the Holy Land was the beginning of a war we all lost." So stated London's *Sunday Telegraph* concerning the Yom Kippur War. One thing is certain—the Yom Kippur War was not the end, but another chapter in a continuing drama.

And as Israel survived the most powerful onslaught yet made upon her, so she will survive every further onslaught. The Lord God has given us his word on this matter: "I will restore the captivity of my people Israel, and they will rebuild the ruined cities and live in them, they will also plant vineyards and drink their wine, and make gardens and eat their fruit. I will also plant them on their land, and they will not again be rooted out from their land which I have given them" (Amos 9:14, 15, NASB). Again, " 'I will make Jerusalem and Judah like a cup of poison to all the nearby nations that send their armies to surround Jerusalem. Jerusalem will be a heavy stone burdening the world. And though all the nations unite in an attempt to move her, they will all be crushed. In that day,' says the Lord, 'I will bewilder the armies drawn up against her, and make fools of them, for I will watch over the people of Judah, but blind all her enemies . . . In that day I will make the clans of Judah like a little fire that sets the forest aflame—like a burning match among the sheaves; they will burn up all the neighboring nations right and left, while Jerusalem stands unmoved . . . For my plan is to destroy all the nations that come against Jerusalem' " (Zechariah 12:2-4, 6, 9, TLB).

"Jerusalem will be a heavy stone burdening the world." This statement has a remarkably contemporary ring about it. The fact is that the Yom Kippur War was only another phase in the battle for Jerusalem. It is clear that whether there is a disengagement or not, some agreement on minor issues or not, there will nevertheless be a renewal of war. Indeed, in all probability Israel is now facing the most terrible conflict in all of her twenty-five-year history. Who would have thought forty years ago that Jerusalem would be a bone of contention among the nations of the world, and that Israel would be the focal point of strife and war? Who would have thought that this little nation, not then even in existence as a sovereign state, and with one-third of the Jewish people having been liquidated in the gas chambers of Nazi Europe, would be the spark to set off a third world conflagration? Who could have foreseen, humanly speaking, that Jerusalem would again become the capital of this dispersed people?

It is interesting that the late King Faisal of Saudi Arabia said again and again that Jerusalem is the real point of contention, and not merely the Golan or the Sinai or the West Bank. The Rabat Conference of Arab nations in 1974 endorsed this view by putting Jerusalem at the heart of the conflict. Now Israel may be prepared to give up Sinai, much (if not nearly all) of the West Bank, and even a certain amount more of the Golan, but Jerusalem is a very different matter. Israel will never surrender Jerusalem. We can therefore see that in the last phase of world history, Jerusalem will indeed be a heavy stone burdening the whole world.

What are the prospects facing Israel now? They are very simple. She is confronted by two stark alternatives—either she withdraws or she does not. If Israel does not withdraw, there will be war. All the Arab nations have made it abundantly clear that renewal of the conflict is the only possibility if Israel does not give up all the land occupied in 1967. Israel has indicated that she would be prepared to give up much of Sinai, including the Abu Rhodeis oilfield and even the strategic passes in central Sinai. She would also be prepared to give up nearly all the West Bank. The Golan is a different proposition, however, as she has already given back nearly all that she can there. To give back more would be to lay the whole of upper Galilee at the mercy of enemy attack.

The fact that the Rabat Conference recognized the Palestinian Liberation Organization as the only representative of the Palestinian people, thus excluding King Hussein and Jordan, has complicated the issue considerably. I do not think that Israel would be prepared to give back the West Bank to the P.L.O., allowing it to become a hostile Marxist-oriented state situated right at her heart.

In the end, it is Jerusalem that will be the real bone of contention, rather than any of these other areas. If Israel is not prepared to give up Jerusalem, there is bound to be a resumption of war. I have found that most Israelis would be prepared to give up the major part of the territory occupied in the 1967 war, if they could only receive in return guaranteed and secure boundaries and genuine peace. Jerusalem, however, they will never give up.

On the other hand, Israel may have to withdraw substantially. The United States has been exerting maximum pressure on her to do so. Since Israel depends upon the United States for most of the economic and military aid that she needs, this pressure is very telling. Golda Meir has said that many think Israel only wants to grab land. Actually Israel only wants what she has farmed for many years. If Israel withdraws, a third world war is inevitable, because America would have to guarantee Israel's frontiers and the Soviet Union those of Syria and Egypt. For the first time the stage would be set for a direct superpower confrontation, and collision would be inevitable.

In early summer 1974, Israel's Prime Minister, Yitzhak Rabin, broadcast to the Israeli people, warning them that war might well resume within a year and that they must be ready and braced for the next assault. Obviously no prime minister would make such a statement without reliable information. His broadcast was in fact based on information collected by Israeli Intelligence forces. As I have said earlier, there has been a tremendous military buildup in the Arab nations, particularly in Syria and Iraq. While Egypt has so far had difficulty in persuading the Soviet Union to replace the weapons lost in the last war and is not up to her former military strength, Syria has trebled hers. Indeed, Syria is now one vast arsenal.

According to Israeli Intelligence the Soviet Union has supplied Syria with the latest MIG 23 fighter, previously found only in the East German and Soviet air forces. The Soviet Union has also been supplying Syria with the latest Soviet weapons. These were not found in her armory during the Yom Kippur War. For the first time Israeli Intelligence has reported to the United Nations that Soviet officers and men are openly manning missile batteries in Syria. Syria has repeatedly claimed that she now has long-range missiles which could hit every city and settlement within Israel. This is not an empty claim. Israeli Intelligence confirms its accuracy.

Since the disengagement on the Golan in May 1974, Syria has been quite outspoken in her newspaper articles and editorials (nearly all of which are government-controlled) saying that war will be resumed. The very demands she is making upon Israel, she knows Israel cannot possibly fulfil.

Iraq has also been receiving weapons from the Soviet Union in unprecedented numbers. She now has one thousand Soviet T54 and T62 tanks. She has also received various missiles, including Scud ground-to-ground missiles. She has been supplied with 350 planes by the Soviet Union, including the new Tupolev 22 long-range bomber. The Tupolev 22 had never been given to any other air force than that of the Soviet Union herself. There are now at least 1,000 to 1,200 Soviet advisors in the Iraqi armed forces. Added to all this is the Soviet naval buildup in the Indian Ocean, Red Sea, and Mediterranean. There are a remarkable number of Soviet personnel in strategic positions at the entrance to the Red Sea.

In the next round of the conflict, nuclear weapons of some kind will very likely be used. It is an interesting fact that every Syrian and Egyptian soldier captured in the last war was equipped with gear for radioactive fallout and biological bacterial warfare. None of the Israeli defense forces were equipped in this way. One cannot help drawing the conclusion that it was expected that such new weapons would be used at some time during the course of the war. On my information, the Soviet Union very nearly permitted this.

We must take note of the warning given by Israel's President Katzir in 1974, when he said that Israel had the capacity to produce nuclear warheads and was working hard on the project. He also said that Israel would not hesitate to use them if she had to. This was a solemn warning to all the nations of the world. It is a widely held view that Israel has an A-bomb, and there is no reason at all to doubt this. If Israel has her back against the wall, she will undoubtedly use it.

From all this emerge some interesting facts. It appears that the real threat of renewed war is now from the north rather than from the south. It also appears that a regrouping is taking place with Syria, Iraq, and the P.L.O., heavily backed by the Soviet Union, providing the real threat. Egypt and Jordan, on the other hand, appear to be open to some kind of negotiated settlement. Referring back to the war predicted in Ezekiel 38 and 39, it is interesting to note that, if this regrouping becomes a substantial feature, we have the first possible sign that the time of its fulfilment is upon us. In the alliance of nations mentioned there, Iran is now the only nation which has not set herself against Israel. Ethiopia and the Sudan (Cush), Libya or Somalia and Eritrea (Put), along with Saudi Arabia (Dedan and Sheba) are all now involved.

In a renewal of war in the Middle East, would the fighting be contained in that area, or would it spread to the whole world? Many thought of the Yom Kippur War as a merely Middle East affair, a localized Israeli conflict. It was not. It had grave significance for the whole world. There is not a nation in the Free World that is not suffering from its economic consequences at the very least. We shall see in the future that very much more began with that war. The Arab oil producers have already stated that in any renewal of the conflict, there would be a total embargo on oil supplies for the duration of hostilities. Many national economies are already teetering on the brink of ruin, and this alone would be enough to send a lot of them over the edge. Thus the outlook for the Free World is dark even if the war does not spread beyond the Middle East.

It is for this reason that the United States has had to state openly that in the event of a total Arab oil embargo, she could not rule out the possibility of a military takeover of the Arab oil fields. I cannot help feeling, moreover, that if the United States takes Israel's side during any coming blowup by means of a military intervention in the area, Russia could well move at lightning speed and occupy Europe. There could then be an exchange of nuclear weapons between the United States and Russia which would leave very much on both sides of the Atlantic devastated.

U. S. servicemen stationed in Germany, certainly those in Intelligence whom I have spoken to, say that the Warsaw Pact countries (i.e. the U.S.S.R. and her satellites) could easily sweep over western Europe. NATO forces could not hold out in Germany for more than a day or two. The Warsaw Pact countries are colossal in numerical strength. Poland alone has 600 fighter bombers. Of course, we do not know how loyal many of these Eastern European forces would be in a war.

Soviet tactics and strategy can, however, be seen clearly in the way they treated Czechoslovakia. They did not only start at the borders. They dropped parachute regiments on the airport in Prague, and took it within an hour. Then the great air transports came in one after another, carrying tanks and everything else right into the heart of the country. This is why one top NATO expert with long and wide experience has said that the Soviet Union and her allies could occupy the Western capitals in four hours by simply seizing their airports. Once you have the airports, you have the countries right at their hearts.

It is a sad fact that we do not now have one strong government in the Free World. Indeed, at the time of writing, Italy, France, Germany, Holland, Belgium, Denmark, Sweden, Norway, and Britain all have minority governments. Even Portugal's strong government, whatever we may have felt about its politics, has now been replaced by a new one which appears to be very shaky. It seems that the same thing could happen in Spain at any time. The whole of Europe is in a weak state, and this is reflected in the absence of great statesmen. Even in the United States, the Presidency does not have the overall confidence of the people.

The Soviet Union has said for years that the Free World would drop into their hands like overripe fruit when the time came. Fourteen years ago it was the plan of the Soviet Union to take Free Europe via Israel, Arab oil, and North Africa. There can have been few times since the end of the Second World War when the Free World has been in such disarray economically, financially and politically. Much of the Free World is at present engrossed in its own domestic crises, and is militarily weak and unprepared. The civil and military leaders of the Soviet Union must be sorely tempted to take advantage of the present situation. It could well be that a further conflict in the Middle East will provide them with the excuse they need.

When we are in our own little Christian circle, we sometimes have the idea that God cannot work anywhere else. It can be very humbling to suddenly find that he has been working in places where, in our estimation, he could not or would not work. I had often been in the Russian Orthodox Church and Convent of the Garden of Gethsemane. It is full of icons, has a dark, filtered light, and smells of incense. In my ignorance, I had never thought that there was much spiritual life there. During the war, however, I discovered that one of the greatest saints in the Middle East is the Abbess of that Convent.

Mother Barbara is in her eighties, and is a most remarkable saint. She is one of the only two people I know of in Israel who had any sense that in 1973 a terrible catastrophe was about to fall upon the nation. Every time that she began to pray for the country during her prayer watches, she found herself in tears. She became so troubled about this that she consulted one of her superiors. He said, "Well, my dear, you are getting old, and when one is getting old one does weep easily." She could not accept this explanation, however, and said later to a friend, "I do not believe it is so. Some terrible catastrophe is hanging over us." She was right.

Mother Barbara told me about prophecies which she had heard in Russia back in 1911. During the political upheavals of that time her father was in danger of his life from several quarters. She feared that he would soon be murdered by one or the other. She therefore went to a monastery many miles north of Moscow, where she knew there were godly monks, and asked them to pray for her father's safety. As a result he and his family were among the few allowed out of Russia at that time. Mother Barbara went to Jerusalem and has lived there ever since. She told me that when the monks were praying for her father, one of them prophesied. She had written it all down.

She brought out an old tattered notebook and began translating parts of the prophecy from Russian: "An evil will shortly take Russia and wherever this evil comes, rivers of blood will flow. This evil will take the whole world, and wherever it goes, rivers of blood will flow again. It is not the Russian soul, but an imposition on the Russian soul. It is not an ideology, nor a philosophy, but a spirit from hell. In the last days Germany will be divided in two. France will just be nothing. Italy will be judged by natural disasters. Britain will lose her empire and all her colonies, and will come to almost total ruin, but will be saved by praying women. America will feed the world, but will finally collapse. Russia and China will destroy each other. Finally Russia will be free and from her, believers will go forth and turn many from the nations to God." The monk also told her, "You will live to see Russia free, but you will not live to see the Antichrist."

Once again I should say that we must not gullibly swallow all of this. We should consider it carefully, testing everything. Nevertheless I do think that these words are quite remarkable. In 1911, who ever would have thought that some crackpot little movement in Russia would rule a very large part of the world? Who would have thought that Germany would be divided in two, or that Britain, then a very strong nation, would lose her empire and all her colonies, and almost come to ruin? Who would have believed that America would be feeding the world? In 1911, who would have thought it possible that Russia and China could destroy each other? Remember that China had only the weakest of governments at that time. If the monk had said that Russia and Japan would destroy each other, that would have been possible. Japan had defeated Russia in the Russo-Japanese War of 1904-5.

While I was in Israel during the war, I had the strong feeling that I was seeing a cameo of what would happen just as suddenly to the Free World. Just as that assault came unexpectedly, so one day we would wake up to find that we were being attacked on all fronts. I believe that the next blowup in Israel could indeed involve the whole world in a very short space of time. Many people feel that if we have a third world war, it could all be over in a few weeks. It could, but in that short time a tremendous amount could have happened. If there were a collision between the United States and Russia over Israel, China could take the opportunity of attacking Russia in the back. Thus we could have half the world locked in conflict within a matter of days.

Within weeks Europe could be occupied and

freed, Russia devastated, and China laid waste, the political systems centered in them destroyed. Very much of what we now call civilization would then be in ruins. Out of such catastrophe could come a period of unparalleled gospel opportunity. It would be opportunity unprecedented in the last 2,000 years, because the world would be in pieces and there would be a moral vacuum. The church of God could have possibilities for preaching and teaching such as she has never known. Then I believe that after a decade or two at the most, there would come a great cry for strong world government, the subsequent rise of a so-called man of peace, the Antichrist, and the final events of world history. In my view all this is a real possibility although speculative. You will, of course, have to test it for yourself. When we come to the clear statements of God's Word we are on a firm foundation. Above and beyond these, however, we must be very careful indeed.

At this point someone is bound to ask, "Will we believers be there to see a third world war? Will we not have been raptured by our Lord?" I would ask them in reply, "What authority have we in the Word of God for believing that a third world war will be the last?" There may be a fourth and fifth. I believe in a Rapture, but I believe that it will come at the beginning of the Tribulation or during it. That is at the very end of the age. I do not believe that we are at the very end yet, but that we are moving into the last phase. I do not know how long we have left. What I do know is that out of the chaos and destruction I have been describing will come the turning of the Jewish people to the Lord. That will be life from the dead (Romans 11:15). The age-old aspiration of the Jewish people has been that ultimately the whole world would be blessed through them, and that all nations would flow to Jerusalem. In the end the Jewish people will see that through the Messiah this has come to pass. They will see that from every nation there are those who are joined to the Messiah, and that in him they have all been made one (Ephesians 2:11-18; 3:6).

Will Israel survive? There is no doubt about it. Whether there is a limited but terrible Middle East war, or a more widely spread nuclear confrontation, Israel will survive. God has said so. Even if all the armies of the world were to gather against Israel, the Jewish people would not be annihilated. Nor will the land be taken away from them. They will more than survive. All that has been promised them will be fulfilled.

# WHAT
# NEXT?

What are the major biblical signs relating to Israel? Many of these have been fulfilled, namely, the return of the Jewish people to the Promised Land, the re-creation of the State of Israel, the possession and repopulating of the land, the rebuilding of the cities which for so many generations were desolate, and the re-taking of Jerusalem. It is interesting to note that all these signs have been fulfilled in this last century, and in fact most of them within the last thirty years.

There are, however, a number of prophecies which have yet to be fulfilled. We know that Israel and Jerusalem will be the focal point of much more conflict, and that further war is predicted. We find some of these wars described in Ezekiel 38, 39; Joel 3; Zechariah 12, 14; Mark 13:14-23; and Revelation 16:16. Whether all these refer to one war or to different wars is debatable. It would seem to me that we have at least a few wars described here, all in Israel's future. I have discussed some of these wars more fully in previous chapters.

It would also seem clear that Israel will end up with much more territory than she has at present. Some would feel that she will finally possess all that God promised to Abraham, that is "from the wilderness to Lebanon, and from the river, the River Euphrates, as far as the Western Sea" (Deuteronomy 11:24, NASB). It would seem that Israel will possess the mountains of Lebanon, Edom, Ammon, and Moab (Isaiah 11:14), that is all of present Jordan and quite a portion of southern Lebanon.

There is another apparently unfulfilled prophecy in Isaiah 19. In verses 23 to 25 it says, "In that day there will be a highway from Egypt to Assyria, and the Assyrians will come into Egypt and the Egyptians into Assyria, and the Egyptians will worship with the Assyrians. In that day Israel will be the third party with Egypt and Assyria, a blessing in the midst of the earth, whom the Lord of hosts has blessed saying, 'Blessed is Egypt My people, and Assyria the work of My hands, and Israel My inheritance' " (NASB). Some would feel that this will have its fulfilment in the Millennium; others feel strongly that it will be fulfilled before the Millennium.

A matter that many people raise in connection with the future of Israel is whether the Temple will be rebuilt or not. This is based upon a number of Old Testament prophecies—for example Amos 9:11, Ezekiel 40–48—and also New Testament references such as Matthew 24:15 ("the abomination of desolation . . . standing in the holy place," NASB) and 2 Thessalonians 2:3, 4 ("the man of lawlessness . . . takes his seat in the temple of God, displaying himself as being God," NASB).

I am not at all sure that the Temple at Jerusalem will be rebuilt. However, some amazing stories about its rebuilding are in circulation at the present time. I think the one about the stone being prepared in Indiana, U.S.A., is absolutely crazy. Israel has got marvelous stone of her own. Can you imagine Orthodox Jewry ever accepting a Temple built with American stone?

There are some very real problems in connection with this whole matter of the Temple. If it is to be rebuilt, are we going to have the reinstitution of the priesthood and of animal sacrifice? It seems to me rather incredible that first we should have the figure, then its fulfilment, then return to the figure; first the shadow, then the substance, then the shadow again. Surely the Messiah has either fulfilled all this or he has not. Nowhere in Scripture does God speak of returning to the figure or shadow, once its fulfilment has come.

The priesthood was subject to very strict rules. If the priesthood were to be reinstituted, how would Israel establish who was qualified for the office? One could take people whose name was Cohen, Khan, Cowan, or other variations on the same name "Cohen," which in Hebrew means "priest." Such Jewish names are a sure indication of descent from priestly families. Has there, however, been any intermarriage down through the years? If so, they would be disqualified. Are there many Cohens who are absolutely pure? Again one could find the Levites through such names as Levy, Levan, and so on, but there would be the same problem of purity. I also cannot believe that there will be a return to animal sacrifice. The vast majority of Jewish people would be wholly against this.

Nevertheless, some people will refer to Ezekiel 40–48 and other similar Scriptures as proof that the Temple will be rebuilt. I am not convinced that these passages are speaking about a literal Temple. I believe rather that they speak of the house of God, and use symbolic language to do so. It is instructive to note the similarity that exists between Ezekiel's vision and John's in Revelation 21, 22. Both, as I see it, are to be interpreted symbolically and not literally. Both speak of the eternal dwelling place of God, not made with hands, but consisting of living stones, that is believing Jews and believing Gentiles together in Christ (Ephesians 2:11-22).

Whether there is to be a literal rebuilding of the Temple or not, what we know for sure is that Christ is building the temple, which is his Church, his Body; and the battle of the ages is over it (Matthew 16:18; cf. Ephesians 2:19-21). I understand the reference to the offering up of sacrifices in the light of 1 Peter 2:5: "You also, as living stones, are being built up as a spiritual house for a holy priesthood, to offer up spiritual sacrifices acceptable to God through Jesus Christ" (NASB).

Whatever happens in the immediate future, Israel will not only survive, she will triumph. I am not the least bit afraid for her. I know that she will come through. Each new phase of strife will be another step in God's cornering of his people. He will corner them in such a way that they will finally be driven to call upon him. Then, in calling upon the Lord, a spirit of supplication and grace will be poured out upon them, and they shall look to him whom they pierced. There will be a mourning that will cover the whole land, a bitterness of heart as for the death of a firstborn son. (Read Zechariah 12:10.) All Israel will recognize the fact that she rejected her Messiah and was party to his crucifixion. What a day that will be! It will not be the kind of mourning that drove Judas to hang himself, but the kind of mourning which Peter felt when, during his trial, Jesus turned and looked at him. Peter went out and wept. This was a repentance that led to restoration. There will be many tears then, which will melt the heart and warm the spirit. It will be life from the dead for the whole Church.

There are diametrically opposed views among evangelicals about the state of the Church at the end of the age. There are those who do not believe that there will be a great revival and awakening. Such people remind us that the Lord said, "When the Son of Man cometh, shall he find faith on the earth?" (Luke 18:8, KJV), and "the love of many shall wax cold" (Matthew 24:12, KJV). There is also the verse in 2 Thessalonians 2:3 which says, "That day shall not come, except there come a falling away first" (KJV). The opposite view, also based on Scripture, is that at the end there will be a great outpouring of the Spirit of God. We are told, for instance, that the prophecy of Joel was not completely fulfilled on the Day of Pentecost and that it awaits a final fulfillment. Those holding this view look for a great awakening, for "latter rain," for "multitudes in the valley of decision."

I personally cannot help but feel that the taking away of the veil from the hearts of the Jewish people will be the complement to the Day of Pentecost. I believe that this divine triumph will mean a tremendous release of resurrection life and power into the whole Church. It will indeed be "life from the dead" (Romans 11:15). This prospect thrills me deeply. After all, the apostles who first took the gospel to the ends of the Roman Empire and beyond were all Jewish. It seems to me that it would be a most wonderful thing if at the end of the age, it was once again those in Christ, in the Messiah, of Hebrew background, who took up the torch and became the dynamic to carry the whole Body of Christ through the last phase of history.

# FACING
# THE FUTURE

Those of us who know the Lord Jesus Christ as Lord and Savior must face up to reality. It may cost us very much to do so, but in the end we shall not regret it. To live in a spiritual fantasyland may be enjoyable for the present, but will not carry us through the day of crisis. In the final analysis it is a matter of spiritual foundations, a subject about which the Bible has much to say.

Our Lord's words in Luke 6:46-49 are very relevant here: "Why do you call Me, 'Lord, Lord', and do not do what I say? Everyone who comes to Me, and hears my words, and *acts upon them,* I will show you whom he is like: he is like a man building a house, who dug deep and laid a foundation upon the rock; and when a flood arose, the river burst against that house and could not shake it, because it had been well built. But the one who has heard, and has not *acted accordingly,* is like a man who built a house upon the ground without any foundation; and the river burst against it and immediately it collapsed, and the ruin of that house was great" (NASB). The Lord Jesus was pointing out that it is not good enough for us merely to hear his words, or even to recognize them as truth. That in itself will not save us from collapse in the day of trial. We have to face up to the truth, face reality and its implications for us, and act accordingly.

I have been a Christian for over twenty-five years, and in that time I have heard numerous references to the fact that we shall see much war and trouble at the end of the age. I have yet to meet a true evangelical who does not believe that the last phase will be marked by wars, great upheavals, and breakdown on every level of life. On the other hand, all of us are loath to believe that any of this could be on our doorsteps. I am sure that when it eventually starts to happen, a large number of us will be taken by surprise. One of the most painful experiences for us as the people of God is to suddenly realize that what we have believed for years might actually be about to happen. Then comes the distress of facing up to all our frittering away of time and money, and our engagement in so much useless activity.

Someone said to me a while ago that we Christians so believe that trouble is coming that we are immunized to it. We tend to think that just because we believe that it will come, we are automatically prepared for it. The contrary, however, can be true. Such a mentality in fact could leave us unprepared. The only answer is to face such reality with living faith.

It is interesting to note that when the Lord Jesus speaks about the signs of his coming in Matthew 24 and 25, he addresses his remarks particularly to the most responsible of his servants, although of course his words have relevance for all true believers. This point is often overlooked. He speaks, for example, of the "master of the house" (Matthew 24:43), and of the "faithful and wise servant" who has been set over the household with responsibility to feed the other servants (Matthew 24:45). He also speaks of "ten virgins," all of whom held a responsible position in connection with the coming wedding. To all of these servants, the most responsible in his work, he says, "Be ye also ready: for in such an hour as ye think not the Son of man cometh" (Matthew 24:44, KJV). And, "Watch therefore; for ye know neither the day nor the hour wherein the Son of man cometh" (Matthew 25:13, KJV).

We would have thought that if anyone was ready, it would have been such responsible servants of the Lord. This only serves to emphasize the need for *all* of us to be ready—for his coming and for trials that come our way. It is worth mentioning here that of all the believers whom I know in Israel, only two had any inkling of coming trouble in the months preceding the Yom Kippur War. It is a sobering fact that the Lord told us not only to pray, but to *watch* and pray.

Many believers, when thinking about the prospect of predicted persecution, worldwide strife, or economic ills, with the attendant loss of jobs and well-being, are filled with great fear. If we become excessively frightened, I think that it means that we have not faced up to the facts. We read the Bible, but we do not face up to all its implications. It is no good ignoring these matters. I am sometimes told that I should not speak about them in this way, but rather give only words of joy and comfort. However, if these things come to pass and take the people for whom I am responsible by surprise, they will not thank me for giving them sweet words of joy and comfort when I ought to have been warning them. There is a sense in which it would be far better for us to have our fear now and be done with it, than suddenly to panic when these things actually begin to happen.

We must see through the negative to the positive, for, in fact, the future for believers is tremendously exciting. Our Lord Jesus did not say, "Be fearful at the prospect of these things." He said, "When these things begin to come to pass, then look up, and lift up your heads; for your redemption draweth nigh" (Luke 21:28, KJV). He described our future in four words: "Your redemption draweth nigh." I believe that we have a tremendous future. There are those who believe that the Rapture of the saints is not far off. Praise God if that is so. I believe that it will probably be a little longer than they think. If I am mistaken about this, so much the better.

The fact of the matter is that our Lord Jesus commanded us to "look up and lift up our heads." That is the only antidote to fear. If we look down, we will be fearful. If we look around, we will be fearful. Only by looking up and seeing that the Lord Jesus is enthroned at the right hand of the Father, with all authority in heaven and on earth, will we become full of hope and joy. We have to be ready. We do not know exactly when our Lord will come, but we do know that we are to be ready. To be ready we have to face up to reality. No one can hope to be ready unless he faces the facts of the situation. We must therefore wake up, or we stand to lose very much.

The Lord told us to *watch* and pray, not merely to pray. The word "watch" means to keep awake or to be alert, and is a timely word for the days in which we are living. We must keep awake and alive to all that is happening, and turn it into prayer. It is interesting to note that our Lord told us to "keep alert at all times, praying in order that you may have strength to escape all these things that are about to take place, and to stand before the Son of man" (Luke 21:36, NASB). In reference to the final phase of the end, he also told us to "pray that your flight may not be in the winter, or on a Sabbath" (Matthew 24:20, NASB). In other words, our prayer is to be intensely practical. Then again, on a different level, the Lord would have us enter into that realm of prayer warfare in which, by his Spirit, we see his purpose fulfilled and realized.

The trouble with most believers today is that they stop praying where believers in the Bible began. What do I mean by this? I mean that usually when we find out what the will of God is about a matter, we thank him and stop praying. Daniel, however, when he found out that the seventy years of captivity were about to be fulfilled and that he was living in those very days, began to pray three times a day for its realization. (See Daniel 9:1-3.) Why did he need to pray about this? If God had already revealed to Jeremiah that there were seventy years of captivity, surely, in the sovereignty of God, it would finish at the end of that time, whether Daniel prayed or not.

Here we face the mystery of prayer. We can pray into being what God has said he will do and do sovereignly. Satan became so disturbed by Daniel's prayer that he sought to destroy him in the lions' den. Daniel, however, came out of the den to fulfil his prayer ministry. We need to know something of such prayer. If we believe that God has said something about Israel, about the veil being taken away from the Jewish heart, and about the Church of God in the time of the end, we need, by the Spirit, to pray his purpose into fulfillment.

Israel has never been in such need of prayer as now. It is interesting to note the exhortation to "pray for the peace of Jerusalem" (Psalm 122:6, KJV), and the promise that follows it: "They shall prosper that love thee." Although it is undoubtedly correct to interpret this in terms of the spiritual Jerusalem ("the Jerusalem which is above"), and to pray for the peace and upbuilding of the people of God, God's spiritual Zion, it also has a physical and literal application. It is interesting to see how that application has come into its own in the last twenty-five years. The peace of the world is increasingly dependent upon the peace of Jerusalem.

It is even more interesting to note the principle contained in the promise, "they shall prosper that love thee." The fact of the matter is that God will judge every nation by its attitude to Israel. This is more than made clear in such Scriptures as Zechariah 12. Nations that compromise over Israel will themselves be compromised. Nations that seek to break Israel will themselves be broken. Nations that go against Israel will be opposed by God.

Towards the end of 1973, a Dutch Reformed minister had a dream. In his dream he saw a square in Utrecht, a town in Holland. On one side of the square stands a statue of Willibrord mounted on a horse. (Willibrord was responsible for bringing the gospel to Holland at the end of the seventh century.) The statue has been there for years. On the other side of the same square is a much smaller and more beautiful statue of Anne Frank, the young Jewish girl who died in the concentration camp at Belsen, and whose diary has since moved the hearts of millions.

In his dream he saw Willibrord dismount, cross the square to Anne Frank and take her up in his arms. He then turned round and started to carry her back to his horse. However, as he walked across the square, his steps became slower and slower until he could go no further. Anne Frank had become too heavy for him.

Then he saw a remarkable thing. Anne Frank began to carry Willibrord. This dear man understood from his dream that God was saying that if Holland stood by Israel whatever the cost, in the end Israel would be the salvation of Holland. This is a vital truth. It applies

to nations, and to individuals—"they shall prosper that love thee."

## GOD'S
## PURPOSE
## IN ISRAEL

There are those who say that there is no place for the Jew in God's program, and that all unfulfilled biblical prophecy about Israel is really for the Church. The Jew is under the wrath of God, they say.

Then there are others who give to the Jew such a unique and exalted position that you wonder why you are a Christian. Would it not be better after all to be a Jew? There is a kind of civil war going on between these two points of view. The most confusing thing is the way in which both parties use Scripture in their support. The more you listen to one side, the more you are convinced by it. Then you listen to the other, and you become even more convinced by that. You end up wondering what you do believe. There appears to be so much Scripture to support both of these views. Nevertheless, as I see it, once we see the heart of this matter, a lot of our problems disappear.

What is the purpose of God for the Jewish people? Romans 11:11 says, "Through their fall salvation is come unto the Gentiles" (KJV). But what was God's original plan? Why did he choose Abraham out of all the men on the earth? It was because he had a definite purpose in mind. He was forming a people. Why? That they might become the dwelling place of God. It was not that the Jews should become merely a separated people, but that they should be the vessel to take salvation to all nations. They were to be the means by which the light of God was to shine in the darkest parts of the world.

Their calling was not to be an end within itself, but the glorious means by which the knowledge of God should cover the earth as the waters cover the sea. The temptation to make their divine election and calling an end in itself has been present from the beginning of Jewish history. Indeed, this was one of the main burdens of the prophets.

Jonah is a good example of this kind of false particularism, which says that everything outside of the covenant people is "uncircumcision," and that God is not even interested in them. So when the voice of God came to Jonah in one of his "quiet times" saying, "Jonah, I want you to go to Nineveh," he became very confused. Jonah was in a theological straitjacket of his own making, and he could not have escaped from it even if he had wanted to.

So he did the only thing that he could; he ran away. He booked a passage on a boat going as far from Nineveh as possible and tried to put as much distance as he could between that city and himself. God, however, had prepared a great fish and a great storm. In the fish Jonah remembered Solomon's prayer at the dedication of the Temple. He repented and prayed, and the Lord heard him. (See Jonah 2, especially v. 4; cf. 1 Kings 8:22-53.)

When he got to Nineveh Jonah delivered God's message with all the energy he could muster. It was a message of judgment, and it perfectly matched Jonah's own feelings about what that city deserved. It was one of the greatest shocks of his life when all the Ninevites, from the king downwards, repented. They even dressed the domestic animals in sackcloth. As a result of this, God deferred his judgment on the city for a generation. Jonah, however, was very angry indeed—"it displeased Jonah exceedingly!"

We can see ourselves in Jonah. He was the prisoner of his own theology. As is so often the case when our conceptions receive a divine blow, he fell into a deep depression and went away and sulked. The last straw was when the Lord allowed a gourd to grow up to shade him and then let it die within a day. God was in the whole thing, however. He prepared the gourd, he prepared the worm that killed it, and he prepared the sultry east wind that caused Jonah to faint. It is interesting that Jonah went out of the city, not because he wanted to die— that came later—but because he could not face up to the possibility that his conceptions were wrong. He went out to wait for the Lord to change his mind, and come round to a more sensible way of thinking.

As Jonah was pouting over the death of the gourd, God came to him and said, "Jonah, you have had more compassion on that gourd that grew overnight and perished overnight than you have had upon the whole city of Nineveh. How can I destroy this great city? Should I not show compassion upon the 120,000 toddlers who do not know their left hand from their right, and the many animals?" It took a great man to leave the book of Jonah where the author did. We ought to remember that when we are tempted to judge the reluctant prophet. If I had been writing my autobiography containing this story, I would have added another short paragraph: "And Jonah turned again to the Lord, and saw the purpose of God in the calling of his people." Jonah was evidently so dealt with, however, that he could leave the account where he did, so that ever afterwards people could speak about his hardness. He left it with a message.

Why did God choose Israel? Jonah learned the answer to this the hard way. Israel's calling was to save Nineveh, not to damn it. Her vocation was to take the knowledge of God to Nineveh, not to withhold it from her. Of course, if you had spoken to Jonah, he would have said, "If they all want to come up to Jerusalem and get converted, that is all right. We will accept them after we have put them through the course." However, God knew the streets of Nineveh as well as he knew the streets of Jerusalem. He knew the number of young children and babies living there. He even knew the domestic animals. That was a shock to Jonah, believe me.

The Lord will not judge even a heathen city without first warning it. What a revelation we have here of the character and nature of God. He has never judged a nation or a city or even a system without warning them. Sometimes even believers make God appear to be a kind of divine machine, with reactions and responses more like those of an electronic brain than of a person. We must remember that God is both light and love, and that it pains him to have to judge.

Why was the book of Jonah written? In order that we might understand that God had a purpose for his people that was not fulfilled by them. That is why our Lord spoke of the sign of Jonah the prophet (Matthew 12:38-41). Jonah symbolizes the death, burial, and resurrection of the Messiah, because only through the Lord Jesus could this original purpose of God for his people be fulfilled. Only through him and his work at Calvary could the salvation of God be carried to the ends of the earth, and an innumerable multitude from every tongue and tribe and nation come into the commonwealth of Israel.

There has been such tragic ignorance as to the purpose of God in the election and divine calling of Israel. Our interpretation of Romans 9–11 is fundamental to this whole matter. Are these chapters a mere parenthesis in the Apostle's tremendous argument, a kind of heavenly digression with real value but distinct from his main line of thought? The Apostle has been unfolding the whole counsel of God concerning the believer's standing in Christ, and has ended with the tremendous statement contained in Romans 8:39 that there is nothing which can separate us from the love of God in him. Does he then suddenly shoot off at a tangent only to come back to his original theme in Romans 12:1: "I beseech you therefore, brethren, by the mercies of God . . ."

Does the "therefore" in chapter 12 refer back to the first eight chapters of the book rather than to the whole eleven? Or is the Apostle Paul, by the Spirit of God, taking us into the holiest of all to face what lies behind our "so great salvation?" Everyone agrees, however they interpret the passage, that the subject matter of Romans 9–11 is predestination and election. The fact of the matter is that the Israel of God is at the very heart of these chapters, and we, therefore, have to ask ourselves if there are two elect peoples. Or has the Lord been doing basically one thing since Abraham?

In my estimation there is only one elect people. The problem is that we tend to think of them as Gentiles. God starts on the other foot. He says that Abraham is the father of all who believe (Romans 4:11, 12; Galatians 3:7, 29). Every Gentile who believes is incorporated into the commonwealth of Israel. So it is not a matter of the believing Jew coming to the Christian, but of his coming into the Messiah, in the same way the believing Gentile has.

Paul puts it like this in Ephesians 2:11-16: "Therefore remember that at one time you Gentiles in the flesh, called the uncircumcision by what is called the circumcision, which is made in the flesh by hands—remember that you were at that time separated from Christ, alienated from the commonwealth of Israel, and strangers to the covenants of promise, having no hope and without God in the world. But now in Christ Jesus you who once were far off have been brought near in the blood of Christ. For he is our peace, who has made us both one, and has broken down the dividing wall of hostility, by abolishing in his flesh the law of commandments and ordinances, that he might create in himself one new man in place of the two, so making peace, and might reconcile us both to God in one body through the cross, thereby bringing the hostility to an end" (RSV). Again, in Ephesians 3:6: ". . . the Gentiles are fellow heirs, members of the same body, and partakers of the promise in Christ Jesus through the gospel" (RSV). (See also Galatians 3:28.) It is in the Messiah that the two become one.

In Romans 11 the Apostle Paul speaks of an olive tree. He says in verses 17 and 18: "But if some of the branches were broken off, and you, being a wild olive, were grafted in among them and became partaker with them of the rich root of the olive tree, do not be arrogant toward the branches; but if you are arrogant, remember that it is not you who supports the root, but the root supports you" (NASB). The natural branches, unbelieving Jews, were broken off, and the wild olive branches, believing Gentiles, were grafted in.

Note that the believing Gentiles have been grafted into something. This is emphasized by the words "became partaker with them of the rich root of the olive tree." What does "grafted in among them" and "partaker with them" mean here? To whom does the word "them" refer? Note also that it is not "you" (i.e. the believing Gentile) who supports the root, but the root supports "you." What is the root which carries the innumerable multitude of the redeemed since Calvary? It surely speaks of the Messiah who is the root of Jesse (Isaiah 11:10; cf. Romans 15:12), as well as the offspring of Jesse. That is why the Lord Jesus could say, "Before Abraham was I am" (John 8:58).

It therefore surely means that Abraham, Isaac, Jacob, Moses, David, Isaiah, Jeremiah, Zechariah, etc. are the stock which carries you. You are not carrying them, you are grafted in with them. You have become partakers with them. See Ephesians 2:19; Hebrews 11:39, 40; Matthew 8:11, 12; Revelation 21:12, 14. (Note the names of the twelve patriarchs and of the twelve apostles, representing the elect people of God from both covenants, built into the one city of God.) See also Hebrews 11:10, 16; 12:22; 13:14; Galatians 4:26. The key to all this is that all the redeemed of God have been brought into the commonwealth of Israel.

This whole matter is settled in what it means to be "one man in the Messiah." Is the Jew saved in a different way from the Gentile, or is he also saved through the blood of the Messiah? The fact is that there is only one work of redemption through which both Jew and Gentile are saved. Furthermore, once the Jew is saved, is he in the Messiah or not? A careful reading of the New Testament brings us to the conclusion that the true believer, whether Jew or Gentile, is found in Christ, in the Messiah. For the true believer everything is provided in the Messiah. It is in fact very helpful to our understanding when reading the Scriptures to substitute the Hebrew word "Messiah" for its Greek equivalent "Christ." Even the nickname "Christian" (Acts 11:26) only means "Christ's ones" or "Messiah's ones"!

Was every circumcised Jew saved? Never. Salvation came to those who had a true relationship with the living God by faith. This is what Paul argues in Romans, chapters 4 and 9. He says that "they are not all of Israel who are of Israel." In other words, within the outward people living in the land of Israel were the true people of God. When the Messiah, born of that stock, appeared on the scene, the nation's establishment rejected him. They were circumcised but certainly not saved. Yet in the most amazing way their rejection brought about the redeeming purpose of God (Acts 2:23; 4:27, 28).

Who were the first people to be saved in New Testament times? Every one of them was Jewish so far as we know. With the possible exception of Dr. Luke, all the writers of the New Testament were Hebrew believers—moved of course by the Spirit of God. We have therefore the outward people of God, Israel, and within that people the true Israel of God. These were the natural branches which were never broken off. The Apostle Paul says in Romans 11:7, "The election obtained it, and the rest were hardened." These are hard words, but the Word of God nevertheless.

We must note that in Romans 11:20, it is stated that the natural branches which were broken off were broken off because of unbelief. Similarly, the wild olive branches were grafted in because of God-given faith. In other words, all in this olive tree stand by faith. All this adds up to the simple fact that while the New Testament declares dogmatically that there is a new man, a new creation in the Messiah, Gentile believers have come into something which has its roots in the old covenant, and is the glorious fulfilment of it.

There has been a drastic change from the New Testament outlook that a Jew, when he became a follower of Yeshua (Jesus), maintained his Jewishness and his Jewish culture. Today a Jew who becomes such a follower of Yeshua is identified as a Christian. According to many evangelical Christians, moreover, the loss of his Jewishness and separation from his Jewish culture is intrinsic to that identification. I think that this is very sad.

Of course there are some who go too far the other way. They are so overanxious to keep their Jewish identity that they contradict their standing in Christ. The whole point is that when a Jew is born again, he really becomes a fulfilled Jew. Whether you call him a Jewish Christian, a Messianic believer, a follower of Yeshua or Jesus, or a Hebrew believer (the term I prefer), he has been fulfilled. Such a one has come into the Messiah so long promised, and has thus fulfilled God's original calling.

There are of course problems here, such as

that of circumcision, keeping the law, adhering to kosher laws, etc. These problems are not new, however. They are precisely those that the early church faced. Indeed, these very problems were the occasion for much of the teaching in the New Testament, especially in the Epistles. Look for instance at Colossians 2:16ff. and Romans 14:5, 6. Paul's argument is this: "If one man wants to keep a particular day as holy, and another man wants to keep every day as holy, OK; if one man feels that he ought not to eat meat, or he observes certain food laws, and another feels himself free from such laws, OK, but such views either for or against must not be made the ground for division." The fact is that this problem had caused a certain amount of division in the early church, and it was this that the Apostle was seeking to correct. If my dietary law separates me from my fellow-believers, it is wrong. Upon the matter of circumcision the Apostle was even more adamant. (See his letter to the Galatians.) It is interesting to see that these New Testament problems are again becoming problems in our own day.

On the other hand, if the oneness the believing Jew has with believers from a Gentile background alienates him from his fellow Jews, is this division wrong too? When a Jew becomes a believer he has been born again into the elect people of God. He has come into the Messiah and into his oneness. There is, however, no reason why he should lose his Jewishness culturally. He is still a Jew in the same way that other believers are still British or Chinese or American. He should not feel more alienated from his fellow Jews than they do from their fellow Britishers, fellow Chinese, or fellow Americans. It is the making our race, our nationality, or our culture the ground for division that is wrong (Colossians 3:10, 11).

We are not expected, however, to totally shed all of our cultural heritage. Nevertheless, Paul saw that in Christ there is a new creation. The old has passed away, everything has become new (2 Corinthians 5:17). All the redeemed, whether Jew or Gentile, have in the Messiah been separated unto God. In this right sense we all know a division from this world and a being joined to God.

Believers, who were originally Jewish, became what we call the Church of God. They were the true Israel of God. The majority of the Jewish people remained unbelievers and were therefore distinct from this. They went on to their sad and terrible history, and the Church moved on to become increasingly composed of those with Gentile background. It seems to me quite clear from the Word of God that in our day we are going to see the two lines come together again. Israel is being forced into a place where she will turn to God, and as she turns to God she will recognize her Messiah.

Already I find more and more educated Jews beginning to consider who Jesus was and is. In Jewish thought right down the years, the cross of Christ has represented everything unlovely and cruel. For the Jew, it has been the symbol of persecution, hatred, and injustice.

Since the creation of the modern-day State of Israel, however, there has been a growing change of attitude. Jewish people are beginning to look at Jesus more honestly. There is the beginning of a genuine inquiry. In the days ahead we are going to see multitudes of them born again through the power of God. What a glorious future we have in front of us. I believe that something remarkable is going to happen with Israel before the coming of the Lord. It seems to me that we are going to see the counterpart of Pentecost at the end of the age.

Sometimes we believers forget that in the wise and never-failing counsels of God, the falling away of the Jewish people played a definite role. For as things were, the Gentiles could never have been reached and brought into God's eternal purpose and saving grace but by the ending of Jewish nationhood and their dispersion. We forget also that we have been brought into something which has its root in the Old Testament, and which carries everything that has followed. There are those who would have us dismiss almost all that happened in the Old Testament. For them, the the New Testament, they say, is something alneed the Old. Apart from it being a good illustration book, it is merely a kind of prehistoric and useless appendage. What God did in the New Testament, they say, is something altogether separate, which can and does stand on its own.

For instance, there is the view that the Church, the Body of Christ, is an entirely New

Testament concept, which has nothing to do with the Old and was a kind of divine afterthought when the Jewish people failed. This is surely taking the matter too far. The whole Old Testament looks forward to the New and finds its fulfillment in it. God's people under the Old Covenant were as much a part of what he has been doing and is continuing to do as we are. They and we are one, the elect people of God.

The glorious truth is that when the predestinating power and grace of God has drawn in the fullness of the Gentiles, then that hardening which has befallen Israel will be removed, with the most wonderful results. Those who begin even faintly to understand all this, realize that they are face to face with the mystery of election, the purpose of him who works all things after the counsel of his own will. This is beyond our finite minds to unravel or comprehend. It was the full impact of this mystery upon Paul that made him cry out, "How unsearchable are his judgments, and his ways past finding out" (Romans 11:33, 34, KJV).

The history of God's people is not some hopeless jumble, nor even the rejection and judgment of the Jewish nation with all the ensuing sorrow, suffering, and break-up. It is part of a divine plan, mysterious and in many ways inexplicable. Yet God is its source, its guide, and its goal. The end will finally be the Bride of the Messiah, the Wife of the Lamb, the New Jerusalem. For the fullness of the Gentiles and the fullness of the Jews will have been brought into one body in the Messiah, where there is neither Jew nor Gentile, but the Messiah is everything in everyone. The dimensions of this purpose of God seem so vast, so mysterious, and so invincibly powerful that we are silenced by the realization of our ignorance!

What we do know is this, that if the rejection of the Jewish people meant the unsearchable riches of Christ for the Gentiles, what can their restoration mean but even greater fullness! And if their casting away meant reconciliation for the Gentile world, what will their receiving again be but life from the dead! It will be nothing less than the finishing of the mystery of God. The prospect is so marvelous, so filled with glory, so utterly commensurate with the grace and character of the God we know, that to me at any rate, it is no wonder that Paul breaks forth into his paean of praise: "Oh, what a wonderful God we have! How great are his wisdom and knowledge and riches! How impossible it is for us to understand his decisions and his methods! For who among us can know the mind of the Lord? Who knows enough to be his counselor and guide? And who could ever offer to the Lord enough to induce him to act? For everything comes from God alone. Everything lives by his power, and everything is for his glory. To him be glory evermore" (Romans 11:33-36, TLB).

## 10
## FROM THE
## FIG TREE
## LEARN
## ITS LESSON

What did Christ mean when he said, "From the fig tree learn its lesson" (Mark 13:28, RSV), or "Learn the parable from the fig tree" (NASB)?

The word translated "lesson" in the Revised Standard Version is the same word that is often elsewhere translated as "parable." Indeed, when Luke records this statement, he uses the word in such a way that the RSV has to translate it as "parable." (See Luke 21:29.)

In Mark 11:13, 14 there is a reference to a fig tree, and then again in 11:20 and 13:28. The events recorded in these passages all took place within two days. Are these references to be understood in relation to one another?

On the morning of the first day, the disciples saw that the Lord was hungry. They watched him go over to a fig tree and look for fruit, when he knew perfectly well that there could not be fruit on it at that time of the year. In other words, Jesus was using this fig tree as an object lesson. After pronouncing a word of judgment on the tree, he went into the Temple and cast out the money-changers saying, "Is it not written, 'My house shall be called a house of prayer for all the nations'? But you have made it a den of robbers" (Mark 11:15-18, RSV).

The next morning the disciples saw that the fig tree had withered from its roots, and Peter drew the Lord's attention to it (Mark 11:20, 21). The end of Mark 11 and all of chapter 12 goes on to describe the final confrontation between the Messiah and his people. This was not of course with all the people, but with the establishment or leadership of the people. Matthew, who gives the fullest account of this confrontation, ends with the severest denunciation ever recorded in Scripture (Matthew 23:37): "O Jerusalem, Jerusalem, who kills the prophets and stones those who are sent to her! How often I wanted to gather your children together, the way a hen gathers her chicks under her wings, and you were unwilling. Behold, your house is being left to you desolate" (NASB).

It would have been a terrible thing if those had been the final words of our Lord to the Jewish people, but they were not. This is where so many preachers have made their mistake. They have pronounced final judgment on the Jewish people, as though these were the last words the Messiah had uttered, giving no hope or future to the Jew whatsoever. The concluding words of our Lord, however, were not, "Your house is being left to you desolate," nor "From now on you shall not see me." There was a glorious "until." "For I say to you, from now on you shall not see Me *until* you say, 'Blessed is He who comes in the name of the Lord.' " This was the traditional and age-old Hebrew greeting: "Welcome in the name of the Lord." The rejected Messiah was saying that there would come a day when they would welcome and receive him.

As the Messiah was leaving the Temple for the last time, never to enter it again, the disciples drew his attention to the magnificent stones of the Temple, and he told them that not one of those stones would be left on another. The fig tree would wither from its roots. Later that same day up on the Mount of Olives overlooking the Temple, some of the disciples came privately and asked Christ, "When will the Temple be destroyed, and these stones cast down so that there is not one left upon another? What will be the sign of your return, and of the end of the world?" He touched on a number of matters that would characterize the end and then said, "From the fig tree learn its lesson" (Mark 13:28, RSV).

It is an inescapable conclusion, as far as I am concerned, that the events connected with the fig tree during the previous two days must be related to what the Lord said here. If they are not, then it seems unfortunate, to say the least, that the fig tree was used here as an illustration at all. Its use is misleading and certainly open to misinterpretation. Knowing the care with which the Spirit of truth has inspired and governed the writing of the Scriptures, it is much more likely that these incidents concerning the fig tree are related. In other words, Christ used that fig tree as an object lesson, as an acted parable.

Surely the Lord, in this statement, was gathering up all that the fig tree represents in the Bible, as a symbol of the people of God. I know that some would say that the parable of the fig tree has nothing to do with the Jewish people, but is to be understood only as a picture of spring pointing to coming summer. They quote Luke 21:29 in support of this view: "Behold the fig tree, and *all the trees.*" They feel that Christ used the fig tree as an illustration because it was one of the most common fruit trees to be found in Israel at that time. From nature, therefore, he illustrated the way in which we know that winter has ended and summer is approaching.

They would say that the lesson is simply that when we see the things he has told us about coming to pass, we know that his coming is near. The destruction of the Temple and of Jerusalem in A.D. 70 appears to support this view. At that stage in history there seemed no possibility of the Jewish people regaining their sovereignty and independence. In fact it was quite the opposite. A.D. 70 marked the end of their nationhood and the dispersal of the people throughout the world.

Yet why refer to the fig tree with its many associations with the covenant people of God? Why not take some other common fruit tree like the almond or the pomegranate, both of them with symbolic significance? Or why not simply say, "When you see all the trees . . ."? It would have been quite as good an illustration, and without any possibility of misinterpretation. It appears to me that Luke here is emphasizing this *particular* tree. Far from implying merely that summer was coming, he turns our attention to one particular tree, that is, the fig tree.

The fig tree, along with the vine and olive tree, had often been used as a symbol in the Old Testament. It had been used firstly as a symbol of the Promised Land itself, of its plentiful abundance and fertility, and of the possession of it (e.g. Deuteronomy 8:8, 1 Kings 4:25, 2 Kings 18:31, Haggai 2:19, and Zechariah 3:10). Secondly, it was used as a symbol of the covenant people of God and their fruitfulness (e.g. Joel 1:7, Hosea 9:10; cf. Luke 13:6-9). By New Testament times, therefore, the fig tree had associations in the popular mind with the land and the people of God, with both the nation and its national territory.

It therefore seems reasonably clear that in the parable of the fig tree we have a reference to the Jewish people—an infinitely gracious intimation that toward the end of the age something will happen to the judged, dispersed, and despised Jewish people. Christ said in Mark 13:28, "From the fig tree learn its lesson: as soon as its branch becomes tender and puts forth its leaves, you know that summer is near" (RSV). Surely he meant by this that this judged people, this people who were to wither from their roots, would still be there at the end of the age. They would in fact "put forth leaves again." Though dispersed to the ends of the earth, they would eventually come back to the land. They would be reconstituted as a nation. They were judged because of their fruitlessness, but here is the promise that finally they would bear much fruit.

Thus the initial lesson of the fig tree is that when we see the events which Christ predicted being fulfilled, we shall know that his coming is at hand. As surely as summer follows spring, and the trees bursting into leaf herald the coming of summer, so will the coming of Christ follow the events predicted in Matthew 24 or Mark 13. The deeper lesson of the fig tree is that toward the end something will happen to the rejected and dispersed Jewish people, and this too will be an unmistakably clear indication that his coming is near. It is not just a question of all trees breaking into leaf, although at no time in history has there been the birth of so many new nations as in the last thirty years. There is a particular tree among the trees to which our attention is drawn—the fig tree.

In this deeper sense, the parable of the fig tree has a three-fold significance. It speaks firstly of the continuity of the Jewish people. In spite of those dread words of Christ, "Your house is left unto you desolate" (Matthew 23:38) and the even more dread words of the people, "His blood be on us, and on our children" (Matthew 27:25), which led to the destruction of the Temple and of Jerusalem, the break-up and dispersion of the Jewish nation to the ends of the earth, and the beginning of 1900 years of persecution, hatred, and bloodshed; in spite of all that, Israel would, after centuries of exiled misery, still be there at the close of the age. The fig tree would be there as a sign.

The survival of the Jewish people through their long history of suffering and dispersion, unparalleled in the annals of time except by the history of the true Church of God, is miraculous. Many other peoples, in their day much more famous, more established, and more powerful than the Jews, have long since been absorbed by other nations. Today it is impossible to identify people like the Babylonians and the Assyrians. They have disappeared without facing anything remotely like that which the Jews have faced through their long and anguished history. The survival of the Jewish people is a sign to the nations that God directs and governs history. At the end of the age the fig tree is still there!

We ought to note here the Lord's words, "Verily I say unto you, that this generation shall not pass, till all these things be done" (Mark 13:30, KJV). Some believe that the word "generation" here can and should be translated "race." (See NASB margin.) They would make the verse refer to the continuity of the Jewish people throughout the whole age—"This race shall not pass away . . ." It is true that the original Greek word had a rather indefinite and generalized meaning. In normal use it meant "generation" in the sense of people living at the same time, or a period of time lasting about thirty or forty years. Sometimes, however, it was used in the wider sense of "race." It may well have been used by Christ here in this deliberately ambiguous way to include both ideas.

Secondly, the parable of the fig tree speaks of the reconstitution of the Jewish nation and the repossession of its national territory. The fig tree cursed and withered portrays the nation rejected and dispersed; the fig tree putting forth its leaves again portrays the nation reconstituted and the land regained. The Jewish people would not lose their racial or religious identity, but they would lose their nationhood and their land. Although the nation would be utterly broken up and cease to function as a nation, yet at the end it would again come into its own. This would be in spite of 1900 years of lost nationhood, lost national sovereignty, and lost national territory. The re-creation of the State of Israel in 1948 against all odds was a miracle. The Jews had been scattered into all nations and had, to a certain extent, absorbed the culture and conditions around them. They had survived 1900 years of persecution, pogroms, and liquidation schemes. They had survived the holocaust of 1939-45 in which at least 6,000,000 Jews died in Nazi concentration camps. This scattered people was regathered by some sovereign and irresistible power, and reconstituted as a nation among the nations.

More extraordinary than even that was the fact that they were brought back to the very territory from which they had been uprooted and where the break-up of the nation had taken place. They were brought back to "the Promised Land" to regain not only nationhood and national sovereignty, but national territory as well. (Cf. Luke 21:24, "until.") Even Hebrew, for thousands of years a sacred but dead language, has now become the spoken living language of a virile nation. The fig tree has put forth its leaves.

Thirdly, the parable of the fig tree must speak

of fruitfulness. The fig tree was cursed because it was barren. Surely the reference to the fig tree bursting into leaf must mean that finally, through the grace and power of God alone, the Jewish people will bear fruit unto God. Truly believing in the Messiah, they will once more be brought back into the elect people of God. This does not, of course, mean the whole Israeli nation, nor all Jews, any more than we understand "all Gentiles" from the phrase "the fullness of the Gentiles," but it does mean the elect among them (see Romans 11:23-25).

It seems to me that there is no point in mentioning the fig tree here as bursting into leaf unless it speaks of summer fruitfulness, especially when we consider it in the light of the earlier fig tree. So we might well look for something far more wonderful, far more miraculous than the survival of the Jewish people or the reconstitution of the Jewish nation and regaining of national territory. There will be a tremendous ingathering of Jewish people to the Messiah. Then all Israel—the true Israel of God, the elect people of God gathered out of time—shall be saved unto his coming.

How can we explain the mystery of divine election? It is the tenacity of divine and infinite love. "As concerning the gospel, they are enemies for your sakes: but as touching the election, they are beloved for the fathers' sakes" (Romans 11:28, KJV). They became enemies because of God's love for the Gentiles, but are beloved because of their origin. It is precisely in this connection, that is, to do with the Jewish people, that God's Word declares that "the gifts and the call of God are irrevocable" (Romans 11:29, RSV). There are few places in the whole history of God's dealings with men where his faithfulness, his love, and his mercy shine more radiantly than here. There are few places where the declaration of that love— "he will not fail thee, nor forsake thee" (Deuteronomy 31:6)—is more amply evidenced.

Can we ever explain God's love for Jacob? Can we ever explain God's love for us? Such love must surely baffle us. "Jacob" means literally "one who follows at the heel," and was used figuratively for one who supplants, circumvents, or deceives (see Genesis 25:21-26). Jacob lived up to his name. He stole his twin brother Esau's birthright and blessing, deceived his old father Isaac, and swindled his uncle Laban, only in him to meet his match. Yet it was the grace of God which triumphed in Jacob.

To him came a revelation of God which was to change not only his name, but also his character. The Lord wrestled with him all night and touched him at the heart of his being. "Thy name shall be called no more Jacob, but Israel" (see Genesis 32:22-32). Israel means "God persists" or "God perseveres." Jacob would never have become Israel but for the perseverance of God. Forever after it was that name Israel, with all its glorious meaning and significance, which was to be used for the elect people of God. At the very heart of their existence and of their salvation lies the faithful perseverance and persistence of God himself. This is also the only explanation for the continuity and survival of the Jewish people, their reconstitution as a nation, and their final ingathering to the Messiah, Jesus.

Thus shall be fulfilled the words spoken by that old and godly Jew, Simeon, concerning the Lord Jesus: "For mine eyes have seen thy salvation, which thou hast prepared before the face of all people; a light to lighten the Gentiles, and the glory of thy people Israel" (Luke 2:30-32, KJV). In these wonderful words of Simeon the whole plan of God is encompassed. "Mine eyes have seen thy salvation, which thou hast prepared before the face of all people."

The salvation of God from the beginning was always intended for the whole world, and the Jewish people were meant to be the vehicle for it. The Messiah came from that stock to be the Savior of the world. God had prepared his salvation before the face of all nations.

"A light to lighten the Gentiles." This was the fulfillment in the Messiah of God's plan that the Jewish people should become the means by which that light would shine to the end of the earth. Even their rejection of the Messiah, in the sovereignty of God, has been turned into blessing for the Gentiles.

"The glory of thy people Israel." The Messiah is the supreme glory of the Jewish people. When the fullness of the Gentiles has come in, then the veil will be taken away from the Jewish people, and they will be grafted back.

The unique glory of all the people of God is the Lord himself. Only his faithful persistence could have brought them into his glory. Even more amazing is the fact that the Lord describes his people as "Israel, my glory" (Isaiah 46:13). Such a statement can only be explained by his matchless grace. When all has been said, such grace and love—patient, steadfast, tireless, and undying—are the only explanation for those glorious words: "And so all Israel shall be saved" (Romans 11:26).